SPAIN

Caren Beilin

SANJAY

"Those cruises are crazy, I was on one actually. There was an alarm and we all had to get into boats. It was crazy, man."

Kristen and I are having a hostel roof special in Seville. Paella and alcoholic punch up here for seven euros. What the fuck. Sanjay has been talking. He's been telling us about going on a cruise and about street food, in India. He's Indian. It's boring. It's not boring but there is the anxiety of enduring something potentially ultimately uninteresting. We both scrutinize, on the roof, the sun setting, "Is this uninteresting?"

"The cruise was nice, man. One of the nice ones, but the alarm went off and it was a big deal. We had to, like, get into these little boats, man. Everyone had to get off!"

We're feeling shrewd. We're two traveling women and a man has been talking to us for some time, on a roof, and yes Sevillano hippies are playing guitar up here and paella is served with alcoholic punch, sure. We're women, we're writers. We're worried, man. We think about precision, all the time, about the problem of going on for too long, about how a woman has to be interesting, or mean something *soon*, or explain herself or demean herself or be sex to be read, or heard. How crucial you have to be, if you aren't one. A man. We think about *storytelling*, about being women, and about if our time, by this story, is taken. Ok, the alarm went off, Sanjay, ok, you went on this cruise and there was an alarm, *alarming*. Italics wake up a word. It's boring. We're thinking, Sanjay, you haven't lived so much, though you are Indian and we are American women. Here we are, in Spain. I am covered in flea bites. Kristen's got a bite on her neck, right on the jugular—it's like a plum slaughtered in the heart's basin that bellied up, dead, right there on the skin of her. You could skim it off, but you can't. Somebody bit her, Sanjay. Do you see this? This kid, this young Indian man, younger than we are we really have to realize, hasn't been around, or bitten. We're women. We've been bitten. He thinks everything he does or has happened to him, because he's a man, because he's a person, is so interesting. Goddammit, Sanjay. Everything you ever experienced is worthy of time? Of telling? This roof? This paella? Goddamn this. Worthy of this beautiful sunset?

"Everyone was freaking out, man. The alarm went off. We all had to get in these boats, it was craaazy."

The sun is setting like it is birthing from its burning bright one (its cunt) a determined knife set, which kills it, and Sanjay, you're, what, saying you felt alarmed at an alarm of some kind in the ocean, on a nice cruise you took with your family or friends, or something? You keep going on? We have things to say, too, Sanjay, things we wish we could actually get published. We have had to become so crucial, so cutting. To cut our own work! I, personally, have had to become impregnated with a grown man in the publishing industry and birth him through the cunt of my burning writing so that he cuts it up and kills it, on the birthing butcher table, on my writing desk in the American hospital, so that I could at least publish some pure blue laminates—clearer than all this— of night with no sunset.

It's not right. It's not right we have to listen to you.

"They kept getting all the people into these small boats, man. It was crazy."

We're half asleep on the roof at this point. We're like the people listening to Marlow in the book *Heart of Darkness*, when he tells his whole story, the whole boring book, when he mansplains colonizing Africa to a handful of sleeping people, other men, on a small boat in an eddy twenty miles from London. He goes on and on, Sanjay does, about the cruise and its alarm system.

And then there's just silence, sitting around. It's like we're beholden to something but nothing happened. He never even finished the stupid story but here we are, like dupes, like women, sitting around in the story's unend. In this eddy. Why don't you end this thing and leave us the fuck alone.

I look despairingly, bitterly, at the dark air, to have been so disinterested, to have feared disinterest, for so much time, with my dear friend, in Spain, the blue air that went white, and then dark, the larkbuttered bread (the sun is dead) and I have to ask, to just end this thing with Sanjay, to take the social reins as I often do when I am with my Kristen (she is shy, my friend), "So what happened, I mean how long were you in the boats?" Just kill it, Sanjay, come on.

"You don't understand. The ship went down, man."

SPAIN

I didn't go for a reason, for Aaron's wedding. I write for none. Because. Anytime I write for that, it's cynical.

Good writing, my worst cynicism.

NIPPLE

My father touched my nipple. Maybe this was an unconscious act but I had to claw his hand away from it, there's that. On the Philadelphia street he approached me for a hug, the first we would have in years as I had decided to let him (a bit) back into my life, because why not, because the past doesn't exist, with a brunch, but in the antecedent to the brunch restaurant, on the street, he reached out and touched my hard nipple.

My nipple is always hard. Either one. They are young and brown and hard and, even, long. They are infamous among friends. They were an embarrassment to me when I was a teen, and now they are hidden with light foams assembled in treacherous space (in Bangladesh)—but when he touched one, they were not hidden. I hadn't accepted being an adult like that yet, buying bralettes like that yet on the internet.

My father reached out for one, and touched it, the hardness, like a tumor extruded ornamental and succulent. Something so suckable to some. So hard that Freud would call it masculine, like they are envious of something round in men, their hard heads. They were like hoof-hearted rounds on the centers of my small breasts, the way small ones won't hang things—where had I gotten them from? My mother and sister with their large breasts hanging. From him.

He reached out and touched one. I took his hand down. I had brunch with him, and his girlfriend.

I started having anxiety attacks, a week before my flight. I was afraid I'd have one on the plane. You can't leave a plane. You can hardly leave your seat. I had been having anxiety attacks everywhere, all of the sudden. I was full of anxiety. That hand coming toward me. I had dreams that I woke myself from. I reached in like God's hand and carried my body out, holding it under the sheets where I slept. I held myself there, woken. I have never been raped in my sleep. I wake myself every time, I carry myself, I do the work, out sometimes seconds before the insert. I won't let it happen, if I can help it, if it hasn't happened like that. I had an anxiety attack getting community acupuncture, just a week before my flight. They put the needles in for fifteen dollars, in a room with everyone, hello.

My heart beat so rapidly that the needles responded to my enormous pulse. They were swaying on my skin like thin thermometers of the very sea. My sister gave me one of her Xanax. "If you're afraid," she said, "just take half."

SHEEP

A sheep is like sheep.

I stayed until dark. I watched the sheep, like living mutton.

They milled in circles under olive trees for shade, at the siesta, the grass graying down, a green undoing on the sloping plane in the dusk like a black perfume—the smell of a fetid swan—being spritzed, in Spain.

Darkness, then blackness like oil. I was up a hill. The black air is more than a darkness. A white sheep was dipped in black oil from a harness.

I AXED THE PIG HEAD

I had the hand axe in my hand, a disinterest, and I blew the head in half with a cut, so forceless, a blowhard slice of an already deceased piece of the food property of this Spanish family, the family who had started this artist residency. I was not the real first artist in residence. A prototype, at discount. It had not even really started yet.

It wasn't memorable to see into her head, too expected. She was too already dead. I don't even remember at all. I imagine the bathhard hollow, but I remember only that it was a social triumph to murder the dead pig, to relish in her flesh the future of eating her with others, to cut it all in two. I axed down some kind of door through her head like *The Shining*, like axing out of my body, my film, into them (their country), into a kind of bathroom, shrine to the relaxed sphincter, and later that evening I was eating her ear, deafening no one and nothing, and people grinned. Like I had gone native.

I could not wear my jeans buttoned most of the time. I was always unbuttoning them. There was so much acid fluid. From all the pig. And blood. I wanted to go home, to (only) walk in the midnightery of the many flowers, lit now only by their only colors, red roses, white roses, pink roses, yellow roses, but it was so much later than midnight when I had the courage to excuse myself from this late Spanish dinner—it was light when I went, everyone protesting that I don't somehow sleep there, in the corner—"Don't go." In southern Spain there is the frequent imperative to not go be alone. It was light but still gray in spritzes all over the air, and darker gray like lithe tombs were sleeping like cats in dark corners.

PUPPY

Before the puppy died to me of having fleas, she brought me a fetal bird she had herself pulled forth. She put it on my desk to hold my papers down or what I was reading. Ponge. Flaubert. No women.

SHEEP

I had one of my anxiety attacks on the way up. I was biking, the bike already broken, my heart was beating. I couldn't hear it, how loudly it beat, broken, because the bike covered it up with commotion, the chain gnawing at the mixed nectar of this sound of churning and of the creaking, like fucking wicker up a hill, like metal wicker in a rolling storm. The air was clear and still. The chain popped off my broken bike (they gave it to me this way, shabby) and I had to stop and my heart was, as I suddenly stood, very loud over fields of farmland and sheep circles like fluffing milling moons, around olive trees that twanged out of them.

My heart was much louder than my body at that moment, and it made me faint, to be larger than what I am, like a million microphones spumy in the trees, of me everywhere. It's too much. My heartbeat was pounding in every sheep volume. I sat down, knowing I would faint, deaf (a loss of hearing accompanies these faints), and then I slumped, fine, in a controlled demolition, but when my heartbeat cooled to normalcy, and my body tingled back up, and time passed, historically, sheepdogs were bounding to me, but they bounded by my body in the end like they were in a different film. Like different ends. Our films slid by each other like two asexual projections in the Spanish air, everyone mostly napping at this hour. There were some clouds, like mutton toupees up there. The chain fixed, and I biked further faster, resuming heaving, without water, with some wine at 2 PM in the summer in southern Spain, in 2011, with more interest in having the strength to bike, to be strong, having been so frail just then. Having fainted. A film slumped on a tree, like colophony.

SANJAY

The roof was spectacular. The paella was good, a chef had come and was personable and talented. Sanjay talked with us about Indian street food, it is so hot and fresh and good. It is casual, just from people. You stop on the road and have some by your car, maybe with the people who made it. It is unfindable anywhere else—"That's all I want, man, to open my own place."

Street food like that in a restaurant.

It sounds like something from television or the *New York Times* but it was real, something he wanted to do and has done.

Kristen follows him on social media, and he's done it, and he's married, he's opening a second place now, too.

He was very nice. He was so nice to us, coming forward to say hello like that, cajoling the chef to serve us more than our allotted punch, which happened no problem. There was a sweetness between them—they knew each other. Sanjay knew him, knew chefs and cooking, and sometimes there's a fluidity between men—you could just ask for something, and if you are laid back and not a hysteric or bird-eyed about it, it's easy to give someone such a thing, it's just something anyone would. We shuddered and smiled, and loosened up, to languor in the ease of this system between them— "Hey man, we can have some more punch, is that cool?"

I wouldn't have asked—I would have offered money or sex. There's a way to ask—I am tipsy, I don't know what I ask, what I ask for, what I could be for—I overask, I ask too much, I wince. There's flint in it. Wincing flint, I'm fallow. I'm so fucking fallow. But Sanjay, man, he just asked for extra drinks, and that's what this was. A second round, on the chef. Thanks, man. We languored.

We loved him then.

Now we speak of him often.

The ship went down, man.

We laugh so much. That was such a good ending.

OSAMA

Bin Laden had been assassinated by a group of Americans working on this mission, to kill him. Not to put him on trial. Not to videotape or photograph or document the body.

American college students, who were the children and tweens of 9/11, and because Osama had been their bogeyman, bearded like that on television from time to time, sitting down and being evil and calm, and because they had grown up never without the internet, and they're predominately white, they celebrated the reports of his ceasing to exist like a bunch of fraternities on game days but at a rally, and they were hateful and drunk and misguided—their hearts had been taken so far afield of complication—isn't it in college you learn about systems, forms, frames?

Idolatry of the king. Idolatry of the villain.

It turns the people into the thinnest air, man. It turns us, really, into nothing.

These kids were so embarrassing.

My country is so embarrassing, and brutal.

Osama bin Laden is nothing. A name. And it's unclear that we killed him, or that he existed as such, as the mastermind.

While I was in Spain, in a tiny town, he was reported to have died, the body unvideotaped and thrown into water, like a sailor. Like Santa Claus's shit brother.

American colleges everywhere (in America) vomited in their

quads and dorms and around their roadways the excrement, the American college children, of what they were doing. Becoming corporations. Lacking in education. Their customers roared, like skinheads roaring and shouting and drinking.

I spoke to my mom, the internet miraculously was working again, because the mayor herself of Aramingo had tweaked the wires, after a week, in the square. In her stiff lavender suit and stockings.

I loved to talk to my mom on the computer, her voice is such a sailor, sailing out to me, the body numb and exhausted and nonfunctioning from MS—she slept, she sometimes fell down. Sometimes I saw her when I was very young, fallen. She had forsaken many things in her life, and had to become this punk, to be punk-rock about all the rest—it's punkrock for some to go alone like that to the bathroom. To live alone. To leave your husband when you've lost the ability to walk, to roll out the door (so weak).

I liked to discuss things over the phone, to feel the sail and flex of my mother's voice, the fucking strength. Laughter heterogenous from her nervous system, bubbles the system doesn't blow.

I told her, "I'm glad I'm not in America right now. It's embarrassing."

"Well, what can you do? They were children. They were children when it happened. He was their bogeyman. It's a release for them. You know, to them, the man who did 9/11 is dead, and that is a celebration."

"Oh, Mom. If they or we want to celebrate that, we'd need Dick Cheney's dead body."

"Stop it! You go too far! That's too far!"

I loved to hear her shout and roar.

HENRY

He was in the bathroom, this is a bathroom scene, though I am not there. I am outside of the bathroom. The door is locked. It is a bad scene. He is kneeling down with tinfoil on Christmas night inhaling cocaine. The outside is Montana, freezing. He's lost his coat and come home almost dead from cold, not drugs which haven't killed him still. He lives in Atlanta.

He had been circling the pool bar, Flipper's, playing pool maybe sober all week, but Christmas breaks addicts. They have AA meetings all night on Christmas. He said (of the bathroom) he would be right out. I said what are you doing. I had learned not to enable your addict and I thought of calling the police, on Christmas.

I stood outside of the door shot through with pain that wasn't mine, impersonal, historic pain of people who love this one person. Addiction combines all of them. I felt that my heart was being photographed, clobbered with photography like there were paparazzi suddenly in the house, on my heart, which was stepping out, for the first time, with this ruthless pain.

Bildungsroman as police state.

IT WAS RAINING

A cloud masturbated against the mortar of a castle—the heap of
a ruin that was in view. To the cloud it was good, to itch its body
obliterating it on stones; its blood (the rain) was white and clarified
like the urine of windows raining from its woolen venal universe.
It rained slant into the balcony, which was covered. The rain wet
me. I was reading *Madame Bovary*, cloud-blood coming on her
papery forehead, on a balcony.

SHEEP

The full moon is like a statue of a scoop of sheep concept.

XANAX

I'm not saying that the artist residency paid me. I paid for it.

On the plane, I took half of one Xanax.

I drooled and dissociated.

I didn't know Xanax does this to anyone. I should have known. I am sensitive. I am a paying artist. I should have known Xanax enters the opposition of what it does in a body where the cerebrum has gummed up the womb, like mine.

I was so dissociated. I was on the metro in Madrid, having landed, drooling and far from the ground of my fucking being. A balloon would do nothing here, no metaphor. I like balloon metaphors but no way, not here. You won't help. You weren't there.

I had to leave you where you were.

No one will believe me, I thought, what half of a Xanax has done, will do in a sensitive person, I'm not Marcel Proust, this is not France, it's not then—there is not necessarily that delicacy in Spain. I don't have the kind of money to be delicate like that. I only have a little bag of money that is a remnant from my time spent in my early twenties with a richer, older person who paid for everything for some time. I was able to save. He encouraged me to put some of these savings in CDs. I was using a CD now, to get out of a situation, to leave Montana, I had to leave where you were.

I came for Aaron's wedding.

It was not a fluttering. I wish I could use a metaphor. About a beloved balloon. I like them. But it was not a balloon spliced into feathers, held down and cut up and down explodes—no. There was not rage. I was very afraid. I came back to myself only in whiffs, first in the shower, putting my hands up and together looking

accidentally like a prayer. I didn't pray myself back together.
A woman should learn some lessons.
I didn't learn anything. Don't take Xanax even half.

IT WAS RAINING

The castle was shameful with meaning. It had fallen, it had crumpled down. It was like looking at a full moon that shames in its plen-
itude—why look at something so full? Why look at it full like that?
There's nothing left to lack, like a castle who completes its meaning
in its ruins, how beautiful, how full. It was shameful. I didn't even
look up. And then the rain coming in diagonal enough to bite me
all over, my breasts. I looked down. I didn't look up from my book.

IT WAS RAINING

There were fireworks all the time in the Catholic and the pagan
spring of Spain and this night as I read against it. I read against
what was happening. Fireworks are the airborne chintz. Fireworks
sound like international war. You do not need much light to read
actually, and the fireworks, I did not need them and they were of
such non-assistance to me in any way at all, the chintz, brilliant

but unhelpful for reading the one book I had brought. The translation by Lydia Davis.

Candle, long and thin, made for a dinner together, orange tower, a daffodil liver on top of a tower, on fire.

IT WAS RAINING

Does it matter where I was? Rilke lived in Ronda he used Spain (briefly) as his personal anti-Paris repository. A utopia. A no place, not-Paris.

In Ronda he wrote: the cloud-torn light of heaven.

I've written as much. He wrote: Shadows of the clouds pass over him as if space itself were thinking leisurely thoughts for him. I've thought that, man. He wrote: He who unlocks the secret of flowering: his heart will rise above the smallest of dangers and will meet the greatest of them, death, without fear, in a weak poem before he really wrote, finally finishing the thing in Switzerland, the *Duino Elegies*. That's better.

He wrote to her: I sit here and look and look, until my eyes start to hurt, and I show the view to myself, and say it aloud, as though I'm learning it by heart, but it won't stick in my head, and I can only think that I'm the type who can't make anything thrive.

He looked at a shepherd on a hill, in a poem he wrote in

Ronda. The shepherd flings a stone to mark out the boundary, to keep his flock from running.

It wouldn't have occurred to me these sheep, then or now, need shepherds or sheepdogs for anything but their own protection. To ward attackers off the plane the slope darkening the hill spritzed with gray perfume everywhere the sheep cooling dispersed and cold perhaps running to keep warm.

SHEEP

My wine could just boil in the bottle from the heat. Apricots were in the bottom. I did not remember a corkscrew and went into an open farmhouse for one, everyone asleep. Like a human wolf. I found only a knife and out of laziness or interest, a beautiful knife, I left with it, a thief. I liked it.

The sheep made muttonous moons around trees near me, white and full. In my fuzzy brain, because of the sun, I couldn't think yet of why they would circle so precisely there.

I ended up cracking the bottle like a wine-egg on the side of the tree if only to lick my fingers and eat the apricots out of the grass and Spanish dust like dried goldfish, full of fruit, under this tree I had come to rest with—like them, like sheep. Ah. Because it's so very hot.

I felt that I would rather die from the sun than see anyone at that moment but I was not in a depression. It doesn't matter what happens. I would never have that awful disease, like mutinous sadness. Like most of my family.

Other people are asleep. My happiness.

IT WAS RAINING

I ignored some revelers who called me down from the balcony where they saw me a little. Maybe my candle. I stayed still as if I weren't there and read *Madame Bovary*, but I remember, I didn't actually like it. I didn't think at that time to look at the form, form as heroine—at the time I thought, in the rain, that Emma was an idiot, and I wasn't.

NIPPLE

I am not lying but I don't know what happened. I don't know if my nipple was touched by my dad. I don't remember it quite. I remember raising my hand up to throw his claw back. It was a soft flexing little claw, a peeled claw. I posed with him later for a photograph his girlfriend snapped, and his fingers reached around my back and embraced the edge of my right breast, they imposed themselves past the surf. You are not supposed to shuffle, with your fingers, past the surf in the waters of your little daughter. I know it.

I dreamed about it. I dreamed he raped me when I was young, but I don't think it happened. I think he reached out and touched my nipple when I was 27. That's what I think. And how I went on, to brunch and to the museum with them. Gustav Klimt's paintings in an exhibition, a week before flying out. You can't absorb them. I stood in front of the colors sliding and they gobbled at me. Like an embarrassment of bird graphs.

I remember learning my mother had MS and learning it was a nervous system problem she'd have from now on (would get worse) this issue of her spine becoming deaf to the brain, any directive to move. I thought (I was 10), "Dumb woman, dumb life, why don't you think about it harder and push your motives from your brain into and along your spine with more force like a French press with more finesse—be your body."

I smashed my bedroom into a ship by setting sail, and I set sail writing a captain's log of uncharted unhappiness, but her calling (she always called to me now, couldn't move) smashed the ship and from my bedroom I bounded out—"What? What do you want?"

A Canadian doctor purported MS to be a disease about codependence, your immune system mimics your letting a man's life and his demands bombard yours so thoroughly, like a wolf, like you have never had any sheepdogs. You let anything into you, you allow it all, a bad husband, an abuser, and you let him abuse. You watch him. Your immune system learns to be porous and to actually crumple, like a castle.

We were watching him, the doctor, on TV together, and she said, "No thanks. Turn it off." She didn't want to watch this fucking garbage. She'd had MS since she was 42, probably a lot sooner, and she worked for Community Legal Services in Philadelphia for 35 years, past her illness, well past it, helping people poorer than her, and she left my dad in her tremulous, perilous body when she was 60, her desire and her denial dragging her from the house as if from a dream. She broke frame, she axed the frame like the door down like Jack Nicholson in *The Shining*. "Here's Mommy!" So she doesn't have to listen to this shit from Canada. And I tried not to say shit to her, though I believe it. I believe that's what happened. I believe he touched my nipple and my hand took his hand down— that's the proof, that I took it away. I had the claw. I had to claw him off. I left this country.

PHOTOGRAPHY

I let the town adulterer take pictures of me in the butcher's freezer. I am kneeling near the hanging pig's cavity. I am wearing a silk nightgown he provides, my nipples like speeding hooves sped into rounds, exposed, I'm being exploited for an anorexic ghost look, though I am living. I'm not too thin, my heart is fine, but the photographs are like I am dead, and thin. They're like my bones and my panic. They compare my deep-set eyes to a pig's rectum hanging next to them.

DR. MONEY

If I have a child I think I will die during the birth, like with skiing. Some people die, people snap, when they go. Something happens to their spine, as soon as they ski. They take one lesson. A child, like a lesson, would not sit well in me, and they, the hospital, would save him, and set my body into a river, of blood, for death.

Dr. Money, I met him on the plane, and he invited me actually on a ski vacation.

Obliquely, he mentioned he liked to do things like this. Back in the states. On the plane we were headed there. Spain was done. He was newly divorced.

Back in Spain I had felt unresponsive to the child, free of feelings about her—I would sit at a desk at the convent, and they'd bring a cuteness to me, like a sacrament, would dip their child down, aggressively onto the fragility of my laptop, threatening to break it with the cute fat of a toddler girl, breathing, their punishment. For knowing my limits. What will kill me. For my breasts of ungluggable small breadth. For not even thinking of having anything, not even cash. Who will give me my money? There would be punishment, extraction for all of this, not least of which would be: my paranoia, my happiness.

BLOOD SAUSAGE

Soups of lentils and spinach and onion—blood filled them. It filled me.

I imagined it was sheep blood. Sheep are like moving bushes of dredding tampons.

But blood sausages are full of pig's blood, I know now, I learned, like the juiced neck of a pomegranate pig.

ACID

My stomach was too full of the acid of a pig's head. The pharmacy had been closed forever. I wanted Tums. Or Spanish Tums. My stomach tore. I chewed like a madwoman Susana's ginger, which is hard to find in Spain, she sought out and bought ginger root at health food stores back in Cordoba, and I drank the juice of a lemon, also hers, an antioxidant, but it didn't work. I was in need of synthetic mastery over me. The pharmacy was always closed, for parades and naps and Sundays, Spain like a sitcom, like a drama, like a film with so many, too many, commercial interruptions, only the commerce is the story that tradition, inanity, culture (I write against you) interrupts—commerce should be there, an enduring vapor, and it is awful to plan, to consider where you happen to be. The pharmacy would not open for days, due to a twist of holidays and Sundays and naps. All twisted up. I wanted something synthetic, like Tums, or Spanish Tums, but now, without anything so simple even at all available, for indigestion, I wanted anything, any drug, out of rage, at Spain, so I took something, the thing that I had, half of a packet of a powder called Frenadol, for bad colds. It felt so good. Like speed. I felt articulate and focused, and one with the sunset. I sat at my desk. I smashed the dining table into a desk, by writing on it. I felt full of love. Drugs are beautiful, they do not end with what they mean, and mean to cure, and what they end, a bad cold, and they aren't the end but the beginning of beautiful writing.

A PRICK

My buttons were undone to allow the acids to travel to my lower bowels. I am thin but my stomach bulged, a pregnancy of pig fat. He was talking about his Spanish girlfriend. She was Sevillana, but she was going to come here, within southern Spain, to Aramingo, to visit him in Manuel's house. The house Manuel stipulated would be used after his death only for artists. The latest artist was this boorish person and he called me Vera, the name of the other one like me, to him: to us we were different and close. Vera and I were friends.

He didn't care. He called me Vera in the morning, in the kitchen, to ask for something he wanted for himself, and he took over my desk. In truth, it was the dining table. I was the one who wrote there, and looked at the sunset from that, and watched films there, the sunset, the slashed breast, the bruised back collapsed on the velvet divan or it's charcoal orangine, the photography of clear hazel fluids ripped on a lightboard of lit mauve—but you took it, you scoundrel.

He went to Exeter and was a writer for *Esquire*. He said, "I love Spain I love bullfighting and the salsa," and was having his own Spanish girlfriend, like a ride at Disneyland with the theme of Spain, this cool and beautiful Sevillana who could not read the cues américaine, that he was an obnoxious boorish person and not sufficiently handsome. She couldn't see this, because of cultural difference, or blindness, or will, though she was an artist, a muralist, and would paint a mural on a wall of Aramingo for something Catholic that was coming up, again, another parade, something that lasts in the night, the wall white again soon, when she was gone—a temporary mural on a designated building. There is white paint. That is why she was there, to paint it, what they'd paint white, a commission, and to visit him, because she was his girl-friend, in the house with Vera and I, and Susana.

But his girlfriend had not come yet. She was coming. He snored in the next room like a breathing condition like a sleeping condition like a roar through the house like everything is wrong, like a beast in the bedroom next to mine. Like his wealth in breath, screaming at us all night. His past. He must have driven the prep school mad, the close quarters, the old wood, they must have murdered him with goose pillows every night, but he rose to a position of writer at *Esquire* and was here, in Spain, to write about Spain, directly, about bullfighting and salsa dancing, in Manuel's house for some time, and at my desk, which I concede was the dining table.

He said that his Spanish girlfriend, a Sevillana woman, would come, and sleep with him in his room. She'd be with us. She would then paint a mural here for the new Catholic holiday—the parade, with pagan puppetry. She had proposed it to the town, in a letter, and would come, for and not for him, clever woman, woman wanting to seem casual like she has her own thing going on, has these other reasons, other art than this art of loving, of boring a future into a person, but he said, this jerk, the prick, over pig head, over its fat like birthday cake squares of pig fat, that she utterly bored him, and he was, in truth, done with her. He said it as if to warn us that this was the case. He prepared us for her visit, obliquely. He said, over pig, "It's one of those relationships, you know, where one of the people is desperate about it, wants the relationship more than the other, and the other one is actually just very bored. Has totally moved on to other things. Do you think you know what I mean?" He checked. He prepared us to understand that a woman was being humiliated by him. He humiliated her to us. He humiliated me when he called me Vera. I was not her. My heart was burning with me.

"I'm sorry she's bored with you."

"No. You don't understand."

"I get it, she wants to move on. She's very bored."

I ate the pig's ear, my pants unbuttoned and waiting. For all the acid pain. I wanted to go home. To Manuel's house. To walk without him so not to walk with him. To write in the salon all evening, to write nothing, the same sentence again, like *The Shining*, just to keep the reservation. I'd stay all night. To have my desk back in the morning. I don't care that it was the dining table for everyone. I don't care to dine with anyone.

SHEEP

The sound of my heart was the sound of my death. That's obvious. But I wasn't worried I would die just then on the road when I fainted there. I knew my health. I knew that sometimes I faint at a thought, had fainted before, in health class, for instance, at the thought of AIDS, and at a line drawing, one time, of a vaginal opening. But there is death. We know our hearts are horribly slightly less than any of the hearths.

HENRY

He was becoming paranoid, focused on our door. We would never lock it. It was too safe in Montana, or rapists are often the people you've already invited. I didn't even have a key to the place. It was always just open but the week before Christmas Henry kept locking it. I kept freezing in my broken car out front waiting for him to come—I'd see his form. I'd see him hunching, his mulling and swollen form. He was swollen with so much want. He wanted it.

I waited for him to come home. He had a key. He had locked the door. And he watched the door at night, he prowled before it in the kitchen, and opened it and closed it. He went out. I only wanted the door to be kept unlocked, I kept insisting. "Stop locking our fucking door." I wanted what I wanted, to be able, simply, to come in to our home, and to fumigate him.

WHITE MATERIAL

I could download a film on iTunes, which offered only *White Material* of Claire Denis's oeuvre, which I saw in the salon, like a living room, an aurora over the castle. I was touching the dining table. I reached out and touched it like that. I touched it as boldly and timorously as touching another pussy, a cock, anything, like initiating intimacy—your hand says yes. Isabelle Huppert puts her hand into the wind while she rides a bicycle, and her fingers flex against the presumably hot, wheel-made wind, and we know, I know, that her fingers would not behave like this in France. She lives for the behavior of her hands. She stays in Africa, in what remains in this film an unnamed country. Denis does not name where the conflict comes. It expels the white people like a splooging. It already happened. It has already happened that there can be no longer this colonial system. The white people were getting out of there, wherever this was filmed. It was in Cameroon.

ÁNGEL

He wasn't a writer anymore. He had been an adamant one.

But he had come to filmmaking. He had given up his writing, for what had happened. He told me about it in the salon at 3 AM, the first evening he lived with us. He had left to his room when

Susana and I danced, breast to breast (to French kitsch) but he returned when she left and with his bag of haikubes.

These are cubes with words on the sides, a museum store toy. The Prado. The Prado museum is in Madrid, where Saturn eats the arm of his son, the doll-length son, in the Goya painting. Saturn has a storm system, skin is this system, the temperament, where you'll find the heart sorted out into a storming blanket of paint.

In the painting, his son's head is already gone. Saturn's eyes are mad. He has eaten his little son, the flute-length doll, whose hand is also gone.

Ángel put the haikubes in groups of 7 and 14 and 21 on the dining table. "What does it matter what words they are?"

He was gentle, near 40 on either side, and he had impersonal sadness, like an angel, for the world. "Meaning, I don't think so!" The sentences were, it's true, immemorial.

When he was younger he took a workshop in Madrid with a famous novelist who stole his girlfriend. She was in the workshop, too. He eviscerated Ángel's work. Ángel wrote a long fiction, a non-fiction, 50 pages, exposing their affair, and the maliciousness, the malicious words of them to him, and he was kicked out of the workshop. And the writer, a Spanish writer, was one he had even admired when he was very young, like an American Brautigan whose books we have carried around, turning the pages soft—paper, if you reread it long enough, turns soft. Writing is a venal universe.

Ángel was smashed into a filmmaker by this writer, a beloved writer, famous actually and who stole his girlfriend. A beautiful woman. She must have been. Look at him.

Ángel was good-looking.

SPECULUM

She had been a photographer in New York. Spain was newer to her, she married a man, Iván, from here. Bipolar (my theory went), she was breastfeeding, so must have been off her medication. This must be the reason. She rearranged the lighting in Manuel's with wrists full of New York. Of fucking photographic failure. Galleries empty of her. She broke a mirror. It went down in a bedroom at Manuel's no one yet was using. I heard the smashing rain of a speculum, her toddler daughter like a young lamb, the kind they fill for veal, standing by the door. "Don't move," she screamed. I heard the scream, the sweeping. She was always breastfeeding. I dreamed I had red nipples that fed her daughter.

SUSANA

Susana had been with a boyfriend who was going to help her join him in his position following cows around a mountain, in Switzerland, to be their follower, and counter. But the relationship finished up. Her sadness about this was maybe evident to me in the way she would tighten the percolator so that I could not use it in the morning, I was not strong enough—even she struggled to undo what she had tightened—so sometimes coffee was not possible. Sometimes I felt so angry. We danced, breast to breast, to *La vie en rose*, one of Manuel's French albums, scratched. He was a Francophile, he loved the French, and was a noted communist in this town that had been a stronghold of communism (hating Franco).

VERA

Vera was attracted to the wild garlic on the roadside and collected it like the hard closed tumor of a sweet white flower. She pulled several from the ground where they lay straggled and bulging and in the kitchen she cut them apart into soup standing up at the counter. She offered me soup. A friendship. Two women, soup-standing around. I wanted to join but I knew. I knew only that this town in many ways was always fucking me over. The ATM was out of order everywhere. The pharmacy was closed when I needed drugs badly. Fleas. I refused her soup with an excuse about having had soup earlier, and she ate it standing while we conversed about art and getting the grants and then she vomited, inconsolably.

You can't get in the way of nostalgia. She was vomiting for a long time in the bathroom, like the past's customs office. There is duty and tariff. It is not a good metaphor actually. The bathroom is like my mother, the nurse-glazed furniture, the whiteflower furniture, the loving sheep shower with the spring rain almost boiling, so cleaning. I am nostalgic for any bathroom but the one in Spain. There was no hot water. This was how things were in Aramingo. Vera was in there vomiting. I stood outside for a bit. It was not the first time I had seen a friend want, against reality, the spontaneous land to be a good inside.

Vera rolled wool at the convent, the converted convent, the sanitarium once, the artist's workspace, the dilapidation that was reviving, that global art was hatching in, at a desk, the wool washed in pools, into piles of cigarette shapes. For hours, all day. No video.

I'M NOT MARRIED, I'M CONTENT

The abuelo's pants were pressed. Anti-violet brown. He asked why I am not married. He walked this distance to ask. I said, "I'm not married, I'm content." In Spanish. He stood with me and we stood together. He had come this far, to ask, up a hill. We watched the wheat together out of words.

DR. MONEY

Dr. Money was building a home in Ronda, Spain, where Rilke has lived, but it was slow going. It had been hard to contract anything in a timely manner. I told him, on the plane, eager to converse in the American style, you have to trick Spanish people, if you are in southern Spain, into thinking you are relaxed, you don't care, before they will mobilize any of your requests. They cannot know you have this watchfulness under your tongue. This focused desire. Or a desire, at all, to be alone.

He continued to email me for years, sometimes in the middle of the night, sometimes to ask if I still had the boyfriend to whom I was returning then—it has been years since then.

WHITE MATERIAL

It was an evening when an aurora tore the sky into livers and spleens. I had been at Manuel's for some time. Everyone worked up at the convent, where there were fleas. They went back up after the siesta and got to know each other better in the twilight of working there, together, side by side, and going then for small beers in the square. When the internet worked I bought films on iTunes. I bought Claire Denis's *White Material*, about Isabelle Huppert in Cameroon, or an unnamed African country but that's where this was filmed, her filmed on a bicycle, loving it. Loving her life there. What she could articulate in her fingers she could not in France. The stretch. The coy and curved stretch. Art. Ballet in the sky, holding the hand up while you bike, putting it there so direct, in the air such a free space so seedless there, the lithe blue space, the outer space of blue sea everywhere, the buoyant desiccate, this freedom, for her, from France. She does not go back to France though the Africans assault the colonial, the postcolonial, presence. She operates the plantation even still. She is more at home in Africa—it is a hatred of France, a home made of hate. She puts her hand in the air, in the I'm not there I'm here. Good for her, and they die there. The conflict, the enough, comes for her and her family. But she puts a whole axe in her father's back. What a good ending. A good revenge for what he did to Africa. But it must not be about that. She kills him in the end disguised in a vector of the postcolonial chaos. Cloak of Africa, of politics. But she's psychoanalytic Electra.

I could cut off his hand that reached for me.

I put my hand on the dining table while watching this film.

The aurora and the setting sun dropped an utter butchery of

marigolds through the fallen tower of the castle just outside, and then lit the yellowy blood. I watched it too as the film turned its scenes, it read to me, and Huppert axed her father right in the back, Africalessly (for other reasons), and I put my hand, my material, right on the table. To participate. My feelings swam into the suffering light, effigy bright like dolphins.

SHERVIN

Shervin bit Kristen. He was Iranian and Norwegian, and he bit her. He liked biting. He surprised her, on the neck, in a classroom, in Norway where they studied. The classroom was empty and he bit her on the jugular. It was a little too far, but everything else she liked.

"It is a total miracle and completely surprising he did not draw blood."

They were planning a trip to Granada together but he, surprisingly, broke up with her, or rather, she saw him and another person at a bus stop in their town, and he took this other person, with his ticket and one he bought then, for the other woman, to Spain, and Kristen went, too, with her ticket, to meet me. And I met her there.

We saw him in Granada. He followed her. He said, "Kristen."

I was there. I said, "Hello."

We had not been timely about getting tickets to see inside of the Alhambra, in Granada, the enormous Islamic palace, so we just circled it, the gardens, which is perfect for a friendship, the rule about it: Don't go in.

Kristen loved Shervin for a long time. She thought of him. He was in Japan, still being a student. He was younger than her. He studied for some time in Israel. He persisted in being able to go there. They did not want to let him, because he's Iranian, and what they wanted was the password to his social media accounts to peruse his private messages, if he wanted to study sociology inside of Israel. He called Kristen from Israel on the internet, because he was so persistent, and she heard the squawking of different birds than she's accustomed, and she wanted him very badly, maybe very figuratively. She persisted in this. She wanted to travel, to leave America, she missed it, but not to Israel, but to see Shervin, almost anywhere. There are limits. I wouldn't go there.

There is the feeling you can get: "I would do anything to have this sex back in my life, this uncanny sex—there is no inside. There is the treacherous surface. The endless exaltation of the surface I suffer to touch." He did not draw blood. He drew her to the surface of herself. The other woman he had brought to Granada was some-where near when he followed her, when he asked her to come with him, to his hotel room, which was surely the woman's, as well, and I was near, too, I was there. She didn't abandon me and our trip for this, which is a rule of some friendships, but I saw him, and I

wondered what I understood. I understand how hard it is to find
sex that hallows and fucks your surface, leaving you alone.

PUPPY

"She is really a wild puppy" was the excuse for not treating the dog
for her fleas. She was all bitten up, miserable, impatient. The fleas
sprung from her onto me, they bit me. Fleas bite, traditionally, the
stomach, ankles, and around the wrists.

A pattern begins. You know it's them.

There was no medicine. The pharmacist who in Spain you
have to ask for everything said this was the work of mosquitos, and
she gave me a thin gel, like a placebo.

A cover-up was underfoot.

There was a flea conspiracy in Aramingo.

Everyone was itching their wrists, and stomachs. They were
sitting down to itch their ankles. No one would say what it was.
But I saw what the puppy's condition caused in us. They would
not treat her. "She is wild," they said. They kept their sweet little
toddler away from their dog though—that was the tell.

Fleas, not mosquitos. Pulgas.

I stopped going up there, to the convent. I would work at
Manuel's house, at the dining table, listening to the scratched

French records of Manuel. And Mendelssohn. The scratched recordings of Mendelssohn, and Ravel. That song that is so mounting, that everyone knows of Ravel, that circles and then comes.

Susana, and even the Prick, went up to the convent. Vera went. They itched and went and got to know each other better. I stayed home. I knew I would. I began to itch a little bit less. I cured myself with this distance. I got to know myself, or I reviewed what was known. I knew even if I went (to Spain), I'd stay.

SHEEP + VERA

I told Vera if you sit on the ground and pee, it will not actually puddle and be a mess. The ground takes pee very rapidly, it has many systems, roots and dryness, waiting to receive all of your pee away from you and its surface—you will not actually wet your tush with your own urine, even if you sit completely down. The ground is like a servant at a colonial estate, so dutiful with whatever you put onto its porch. It sweeps your piss-luggage inside with the alacrity of a forced servant in the heat. And it is better to relax and just sit down completely when you pee, if outdoors—when did this crouching thing even begin, when the ground is so goddamned obliging? So forced to bear us? Who told us to crouch, who told you personally to stay off of this earth?

"Vera, you can just sit down. It's a trick I've learned."

Woman to woman.

The ground is so good. The earth is actually obliging.

We peed in places close to where we'd be sitting, with some wine we couldn't get open.

I smashed the bottle against the olive tree, with rage (at alcoholism) and the ground took it, too, and the wine, which was regretful not to drink, left a little blood moon in the dust. We sat on the surface of so much, the sheep so circular under olive trees everywhere, looking like moon sweaters laid out but untenably for the moon with no real reach.

SHEEP + VERA

The sheepdogs scared her, or made her feel fear, more than they should have. They are not meant to provoke fear in even sheep attackers. More, they are bounders bounding out a boundary. They are conductors, they conduct the hill, the strings of green grass, and wouldn't bite shit. They don't bite, they bound.

But Vera was fearful about them as though they were wolves, or she was afraid of dogs. It is alright. Of course it's alright. It's alright, they won't hurt us. It's alright you fear they will. They might. Anything might hurt. Why wouldn't it? Why wouldn't I hurt you?

IT WAS RAINING

Madame Bovary is nothing if you don't look at the form, the fun-house of clauses that adulterate against one another, are different, perform differences in the same sentence. I read outside, on the balcony, in the evening. Nothing else doing in this small town in the rain, in this house where I was initially prototypical and alone. Its socket sucked my laptop so flaccid when I came. The house did not take to my adapter well. My life was in there and dead. The electronics shop—there spontaneously was one—said they would order what I needed. In Spain, everything does get done. Everything comes. It comes when you're over it, when you've started to write on Manuel's old envelopes, and like to, when you begin to appreciate who you don't know any more by virtue of a computer sucked hollow.

Once you've changed, Spain will fulfill all electronics orders.

It was raining. I had no raincoat on. That's not how this works. I had only one book. It was the only book I had in English, translation by Lydia Davis. But it's French. But I couldn't really read it, not right. I kept like an idiot reading plot.

SPECULUM

She was not like me. We were different women. I saw a photograph she had taken of herself during the New York days, nude and in a hat, for art, and I asked, maybe by accident, "Who is this guy?"

"It's me."

I have been misgendered all of the time, am a boy to many types of strangers. It comes up. "Young man!" In this way we had something in common, though I don't know if she'd ever been misgendered before I mistook her. Maybe I aggressed.

She came into my house, the house of Manuel, and smashed the largest mirror.

FLEAS

Flea bites will swell but subside but—you want to open them. What itches calls. It called to me in the shower under all that hot water.

The hot water finally arrived, when I did not need it any longer, when I was dirty and cold and daily. I didn't want.

Then a man came and installed a hot water system into Manuel's house suffering from having been empty these eight years without him. Waiting for the artists of some kind, his stipulation. Any kind of art.

By the time a man came for the shower, when I had convinced

everyone and everything that I didn't give a shit, about hot water, I didn't. I was clean. I didn't love.

SUSANA

Why is the percolator so tight? I can't open it.

Everyone—Susana, Ángel—had already gone up, having walked and broken-biked up to the convent, once the sanitarium. To go be there. The artist's workspace. They were delineating, in the big yard of hardest, baldest dirt, a labyrinth in the Christian mystic tradition, a path for walking meditations. These labyrinths look like parasites, stuffed into circles. And they were planting potatoes in plots, cracking open the dirt. Everyone could help out. Artists could be farmers, mystics. There were beers, and lunch for hours. I liked that they had left, and reveled in Manuel's empty house, cold and boring and free, but I wanted coffee badly.

Why this? Why tight?

What anger transmits to the percolator when you are done with it, with your coffee? What happened to you?

Susana: Impoverished Spanish artist, photographer, taking pictures in the dark, of ghosts. Light is the ghost that comes with time. Susana's long exposures, and then developing them on rags of lampshades, old papers of Manuel's. These pictures of all these women.

Legs. The light of their skin only suffering, with time, to appear, a little. I wanted one. I tried to buy one, but it became stultified. We had a few conversations about how Paypal works, about how I wouldn't be there any longer, when I paid her, I'd pay her later. What would she then, mail me it? I wanted it, one in particular.

I wasn't angry at Susana. I was angry at the history of a percolator, which has long twisted against its own people. Someone twists it but history is twisting them to twist it this tight. I wanted to know what coursed through her arms that did this to us in this house, that tightened us all against coffee when it was wanted, in the morning, or deliciously post-nap at 6 PM, to start the night, there being no other option in Spain, so Spanish. No French press. Goddammit. This wall. My screaming trying wrist. To untwist this thing. Because when I asked her to undo what she did, when she came home from the convent-workspace for a nap, or when she finally fucking woke, and my voice wavered with casual bullshit, she could not.

A PRICK

He was making calls to bullfighters who he felt were elusive and, causally, interesting. They returned his calls promptly, utterly non-elusively, in the middle of Manuel's house. He behaved as if he were being paid enough to live, and travel, and love. He took his calls loudly from bullfighters seriously, like work. He worked at my desk.

When I attempted to play in the salon a scratched Mendelssohn, over which to make breakfast and to prove to this prick this was my house, he turned the record player off and played Mendelssohn for me on his Mac from which he continued his dreadful work, at my desk.

I could not untwist the percolator. Susana had gone up. Ángel had not yet arrived. I hated this prick, I couldn't ask for his strength.

I AXED THE PIG'S HEAD

I axed it in two with Bruno as my guide. He told me to lift the axe and drop it on the line already cut, the demarcation. Drop right in there and keep pressing strong. The pig was dead, man. This was just its head on a stone, outside, ripe for splitting for barbeque, for breaking it down. It was tradition more than anything, to eat the head, but tradition develops into meat in your mouth, like a heavy photograph.

Bruno was on the run from Chile. He showed up here, a visitor to his daughter (the photographer who smashed the mirror). He was trying to marry a Spanish citizen before his three months ran out, pursued poor Susana. He sat by her. He was kind to her, like a pig. Like she had already been cut, and he pressed her.

VAULT

A month before my flight from Philadelphia, I slept in a vault. It was a vestigial bank vault in the funhouse loft of my rich older ex. He let me live there all March. It was an abandoned place, him with his girlfriend in Boston. I avoided the bed, and I had to keep the place—the funhouse, paints and books, no drapes—clean of my hairs. His girlfriend, his fiancée, I think, could not know, she'd be annoyed—a resident in psychiatry at MIT, clotheshorses, both of them, their bonding, look at their clothes, look at them, and she'd later cut all of his including shoes into pieces and in a bag leave them, like leaves.

He said it was like a bag of 30,000 dollars.

I don't think she ever found out I stayed at the loft, and she won't find out. A book is like a drape.

But I slept in the vault out of respect.

In there: a cot from World War II on an oriental rug, and boxes of my books from years ago when I was with him for some time, some of my first joys in those two boxes. A teenager when I met him. Beat poetry.

"Vast, Glowing Vault" is a Paul Celan poem, and it ends, "The world is gone, I must carry you." A good ending.

HENRY

I walked into Anne Marie and Ben's unlocked apartment while they were out getting drunk, a goose in the oven. I sat down. It was nearly time to eat on Christmas night. Ben had hunted it. Anne Marie was writing a novel about Missoula, Montana, burning the fuck down. Burn it down.

They came back. I told them what was going on in my bathroom at home. And, I didn't want to Jack Nicholson into there, to axe the door of the bathroom like Jack Nicholson in *The Shining*, who in *The Shining* was an alcoholic in a lot of sober pain—is one interpretation. I had no force, no axe. And I was being somehow photographed all over by a demon who took pictures of my pain for demonporn, loving someone like that. A fiend. I couldn't get into our bathroom.

Ben pulled the goose from the oven—like an antique turkey, leaner and elegant, it was covered in pepper like any sentence I could have written about what happened with Henry, just their ends were all here, dark, big and burnt, maimed and different, were ragged pepper, all over the goose this butter bright, burnished and burned bird, hunted, wild with its flesh venal with marigold vinegar.

BLOOD SAUSAGE

Ángel arrived as I prepared more blood sausage—it was black—in a lentil soup. I did not yet know what it was. It was delicious.

Ángel told me it was blood. Congealed with little fat cubes but no meat. Blood wrapped in a crinkled hood, it crinkled to be cut. I chopped it up and put it in soup. I offered Ángel some when he came, the first night, from Madrid. A videographer. A Cancer. A vegetarian. He frequently filmed the ocean, the social beaches of the Mediterranean, old men in thongs, gazers and gliders, the surf for long durations. His game was all duration, to let a thing—ocean, bag, person, farm equipment—manifest the stretch and style of its relation and its pattern, and to show how still he felt. He could stand there.

He ate the soup. "I'm a vegetarian, but still." It was like the blood of his childhood. For a Spaniard, it would have been and he was. But he was so quiet for a Spaniard, so reserved. When Susana and I danced in the salon to the French records of Manuel, to *La vie en rose*, he promptly left the room. It was too much, a shamefully full move, too much a friendship-dance to be one. He was a vegetarian, and he maintained that he remained one, having had no meat but fat, and blood.

SHEEP + VERA

Vera was so panicked I was fainting like that. Just like that, controlled and unavailable, away in my weakness, against a tree. It was my panic at having a heart that was beating that hard and loud like the clouds (the evanescent sheep bowels) were nothing but heartbeat bags for only one heart, mine. We had been biking uphill in the utter silence of siesta time, so it beat quite loud. There was no one anywhere. I was getting some needed exercise from all my sitting around, watching films, some heart acceleration under the siesta sun, like a loosening scoop of fire.

I told Vera I was ok. "From time to time I faint," I tried to explain it. I'm one of the fainters you've heard about. Some do faint. Sometimes, Vera, I feel my body chasing me down a corridor very narrow and I'll faint if it touches me.

I tried to explain myself but Vera was sure I had a serious medical problem I should get checked out, like MS.

She said it didn't seem ok how I had to slump there while she fixed my bike. She was capable.

"It's what happens sometimes," I tried to explain.

I wanted her off this worry. I wasn't sick. I was a fainter, and more, I had fainted at a thought. My body was out of sight. If it fainted, it was thought fainting in it, and it stretching out, like a divan, a fainting cushion, for this thought that could not at that moment stand or sit.

I assured her, "I'll be ok in a moment. I'll be right back."
I went to my weakness. I touched my mother underwater.

FRENADOL

Kristen and I took it in our coffee. I put the white powder like de-hydrated sheep concept in the lattés they brought out at the hostel, a new deal in Málaga. You could get two lattés. I buzzed on it, and I rejoiced to be out of Aramingo after months, flowers louche on the beach. They were as big as parasols with their petals, or was it Frenadol? Were the petals small? Was the beach full of boards, boarded up? Were the flowers hard garlic?

I'M NOT MARRIED, I'M CONTENT

Crumpled, medieval, like a mortar elephant bombed out, the castle is too full. But I was bored. It was so boring to be there, to be whole. Why stay? I had paid too much. I had, like an artist, prepaid.

So bored I walked to see it from the other side, along a road before the wheat all around it. I looked and looked, like porn, so boring. Like medieval porn. The sunset came intrepid I remember like a trousseau of butter rats running in the wheat—there is nothing called wild wheat. It was straw or parched chlorophyll on an un-farmed mound, the castle like a medieval anti-silo fallen and so stone still, stuck on the hill so, most of the stones still stuck together.

No wonder the Prick was bored with his Sevillana girlfriend. The minute she got there, to Aramingo, she had him walking her up to the castle, the most obvious place to take romance on a walk. She walked their romance like a dog there. She took photographs of it and painted it later into her mural.

She shouldered, proudly, his expensive camera. She carried herself like him a little. They were good together. He was not bored with her at all. She pleased him with her compliance and interest and hardy beauty. She was, like things he loved, Spanish, yes? He only humiliated her to humiliate himself, to exalt her, because she was finer and she understood him she could read like braille his pain, to be dropped off by his parents at Exeter like that, for the whole year.

The castle became black in the sunset, a silhouette of devastating meaning.

SHEEP

I creaked so loudly on my broken bike my Rocinante into the green country. Olive trees were all over and sheep like living wool mules, carrying wool everywhere like an idiot for other people.

A windmill is a windmill is a windmill.

Pretty smart actually, to trade hair for your life.

VERA

Light coming hard on a book, do you know it? It scours it. It scours and dries the book's bodies, the breasts. The fruit in the book dehydrates. The apricots are dead. Light it pulls the plug, dehydrates and compresses the pond of plot and meanings into a leaf.

Light on a book, do you know this pleasure? Paper stuffing itself with surface I suffer to touch, and I suffer to desire the guts. I've wanted guts, and depth, your liver in the deep water. Your heart down in there. The heart of a story. But nothing gets under book paper. It stops all the Spanish light like a wall a bull fights, a marigold bull the bright horn flat.

Vera lent me her favorite book, and it was falling apart. Reread all the time and carried with her to Spain, it had not softened at all from being profusely referenced and reread but stiffened with water spills and was cracked off the spine—you had to keep it in order, to respect her. She loved this book so much. She traveled everywhere with it. It was the book she brought.

Seeing Is Forgetting the Name of the Thing One Sees: A Life of Contemporary Artist Robert Irwin.

IT WAS RAINING

When Emma Bovary is dead the body vomits black liquid "of some kind" and two people, a pharmacist and a priest, bracket her, observing the cadaver (she looks so lifelike, still vomiting). It was raining like the liquid of dead incandescence.

PHOTOGRAPHY

He said, "Take off your bra" in the freezer.

Everyone said, like it was cute, that he (a local photographer with a wife and several daughters) had a "big crush" on me. He had a big crush, they concurred, on skinny women.

Skinniness combines us.

I took off my bra. My hard nipples were black inside the silk of his daughter's pajama or dress-up slip. He had brought black lipstick for me to put on my mouth. My nipples made for his photographs dark zones of hard interest knots. There is darkness and even balsamic black the harshly bludgeoned mauve.

The photographer sent me these pictures later of myself in his lipstick like that, like I was death or dead, a dead woman near dead pigs, for whatever it's worth, the nipples so advanced with stoniness to be cold like that in the meat freezing environment, making a hard dark break in the silk.

The photographer wanted me to put a finger into the scoured, vaunted rectum of the pig hanging there at eye level. It was an incredibly clean and vacuous black tunnel, butcher-perfected. He wanted my whole fist in her ass. He wanted me kissing the rim, little sweet kisses like a daughter. I was at the end of my time in the town of Aramingo, and I had been avoiding all kinds of events. So I agreed to be photographed. I had been invited camping in a Catholic procession into the mountains. I didn't go. Many of the young people left, to camp at the tip of the process. The internet was out, the stores locked, and that percolator was tight. It was raining. I put my hand on the dining table that evening, the special evening when everyone was gone, doing nothing not writing. I burned a candle for myself, and for Kristen. I wrote to her that evening, the internet flocked off again for the entire week. I wrote with hope, and faith, toward our meeting in Málaga soon and sent her my love in an email inside of myself like I was a cyborg sweetened with help metals. I sent a copper dolphin to Norway.

I couldn't wait to see my friend, Kristen. I was becoming helpless, sad, and too, too nervous in this town. I was in the butcher's freezer the day before I would attempt to take the bus out with no cash, and I didn't get into it, no complainer, I took off my bra like a sweet dutiful daughter of photography, but sheepdogs rightfully filled my fingers, my fist, and I wouldn't go in there. I didn't go right into the pig rectum because I didn't believe it was a tunnel to Kristen.

SUSANA + OSAMA

I told Susana who did 9/11. I told her, over Spanish dinner at 2 AM, about Building 7 which blew up, too, for no reason (a controlled demolition) and what the firefighters said, what everyone said, the architect, "a controlled demolition," the buildings down, man, from their insides, and one of our poets, Amiri Baraka, who died on his sour note with the poem suggesting 9/11 was an inside job: "Who told 4000 Israeli workers at the Twin Towers to stay home that day," he wrote, but didn't die right when he wrote the poem "Somebody Blew Up America" but he died with it, buried himself in a sour stone, which is a good way to die he might have imagined, considering what death does: it comes from above like the MOVE House bombing or from the bottoms of our buildings, like a controlled demolition, so I will die why not in the rolling tomb of my own writing, and they'll bury me for saying it but so what? I was born dead, a cadaver I carry still and all I've got is black vomit.

To Susana, I said, "It was an inside job, man."

I was being aggressive, angry at her. About the percolator and also, the lighter. She took the stove's little lighters away from the house to smoke her cigarette up at the convent. The lighters were all up there. I can't use the stove or the percolator. That's too much. I went to the store to buy a new lighter, it was closed. There was walleyed metal locked over the windows. I wanted to light the stove. I didn't go to the convent any longer. The puppy, her fleas.

I hated it here, there. Her anger tightened the fucking percolator. I tried to make coffee, it transmitted to me. It filled my wrist, the anger. I was angry, too, angry with her, our angers rubbed breasts to kitsch, *La vie en rose*, it was so fucking much.

There was no plane, I told her, at the Pentagon, no photograph, and now none, too, of Bin Laden. We didn't kill him.

"I know," she said, over bread she ate like a robust artist, ripping it, "Amiri Baraka, and that poem. I've read it. Most people in Spain know about 9/11. Did you know that AIDS is a bacteria?"

SHERVIN

Shervin sent Kristen a stone. She brought it out to me, at her house in Oakland. It was years since Norway, and Granada, and I was near the end of my visit. The stone was immutable on the table, like that. From an Iranian desert.

He kept biting her with stone teeth like the bite of a castle.

I AXED THE PIG HEAD

I wasn't depressed I was paranoid I wasn't paranoid I was perceptive. I perceived I was needed to axe into this head, to promote festivity in this vessel. I wasn't a vessel I was writing. I couldn't learn Spanish. I couldn't be there I was here.

LOOD

Samuel sent me a stone. It was a stone from the woods, and he picked it up the night he walked in the woods after reading my letter.

I had sent to him (from Salt Lake) Marguerite Duras's *The Lover*.

I had invited Samuel (four years earlier) to come to the convent in Spain, when he was in Germany, and I said nothing about fleas only, come. As if for sex, that's how it sounded, to me, and he didn't do this. He soundly said he'd need to be paid. He wouldn't pay to be anyone's artist.

We had been, for a book, commissioned.

Four years later he had sent the stone to Utah, still my friend after I had embarrassed myself perhaps to ask if he would come to Spain and put the tonic of our letter-fermenting friendship into my cunt, to shock it. The commission was over, a bust, a shame. Maybe it was even a sham. In our shame to be off the commission, I'd said, "Come here, to this convent," and, well, he did not.

Years pass and he sends me a stone, because I had sent (because of how it ends) Duras's *The Lover*:

And then he had said it to her. He had said that this was as before,
that he loved her still, that he would never be able to stop loving
her, that he would love her until he died.

Despicable weakness, Marguerite, to end a book like this. A
book. I will love you until I die, a spoiled ending.

You are exhausted with writing this, Duras, with being so
good at walking these hoops out into the field, fecund (a dead
brother) (a wild brother) (a foreign place) (the French are elsewhere
again, in Saigon) (the girl womans) (her Chinese lover) and are
seeking now the desolation the desert of a deadening cliché. I will
love you until I die.

Duras, she walks away, before the book ends, she's already
gone, man, to have killed her own book like this. Slap of such a
sentiment. Murder. I will love you until my death, the dead language. The aggressive mask. I sent it to Samuel for these reasons.
Because it made me weep.

SHEEP

A sheep is like a time-lamb. Lambs are just so young. It felt embarrassing to watch circles perfecting on the slope like that, the dark
slope a gray cryptogamy on the green earth and in the air, fume

of uncoloring. As it grayed like mold the sheep, cooling down, loosened and dispersed across all the black grass. Lambs appeared, because they had been folded into the inner circles, because they are children. The grayness then opened its reputable anus. It was black all over in the air. We biked back, down all over, all ways were down now. Everything felt so soft. The stars got fat on lark-butter, I'd like to kill a star to eat its dark buoyant lard. Stars like sheep pepper. Vera's hair the witch.

SPECULUM

She came to the house unannounced, to fret about and to fix the lights, her little daughter toddling.

"We had to incinerate so many newspapers." Manuel was a hoarder.

She went into the bedrooms quickly, in and in, down the hall, penetrating the house wherever, in my room, Manuel's, rearranging. She moved mirrors and one smashed, the large one.

The salon had been very pale and still, the placid marble and the sun, all mine in the afternoon. No one yet had come. Papers out. Ponge. *L'espace littéraire*, I had ordered it from UK Amazon. Samuel sent the Ponge. There were no women yet. I wasn't there.

My gender was like thrush though when she entered, I helped

with her daughter. I held this sweet toddler back, the floor sharpened with so much mirror, the secret silver belly all over the floor. You could see her.

LOOD

Samuel wrote to the Swiss photographers who were based in Berlin, to say he was very sorry (politely) that they thought we had failed, the both of us, so much, to write the prose to accompany their fourth photography book.

We had trouble (Samuel didn't say it, polite) becoming inspired by such pictures, that were like negatives of bowls and rods and poles like a teenager's first engagement with a modern photography lab where chemicals meet paper. Negatives of forks and things.

In our un-inspiration and our vast aggression, and because we were cross continent and had only now met online (we'd been paired up), we wrote each other only love letters for months and sent it to the Swiss this correspondence. We said something like, *The negative presence in the photographs, the negatives, recalls the absence that generates love affairs.* We tried to fall in love. To see if love could be stirred by letters. Samuel wasn't on the internet. I didn't know what he looked like. It had nothing to do with their photography.

They said we'd really embarrassed ourselves.

We had not missed the point of their photographs, which had been sent to me by dossier, but we had not even considered them, at all. In their email they insinuated that our love was immature, like teenagers. Shame could not have been brighter. It flared from every object, from the fetal bird the puppy pulled, and the falabella flared on the side of the hill. On the internet I can learn now the photos were not negatives but the first resonances of object light captured by direct positive paper, but we could not see this at all. Me nor Samuel. They were too boring. This Swiss shit, it didn't dance on a cadaver of the born dead like good art.

They said they wanted the digits to my bank account, to pay me for half of the commission, for my time. I pursued a need in my mind for this all to have been a big scam. The money never came. I didn't think it would. Did they take mine? Is there money?

I pursued Samuel in reality, I said he should come to Spain, from somewhere in Germany. I didn't really know. I needed, with the fucking, to smash shame, to be penetrated beyond the *Light of Other Days*.

MURAT

Murat slept in the hostel, in Málaga. Kristen and I administered our Frenadol powder into lattés, walked the beachfront, had white wine, and men followed us, especially because she carried a pink parasol like a rectum. Murat, no matter what, was asleep.

He woke and told me, in a 30-minute period, he had studied filmmaking in Chicago and would return to the states to become a nurse. He went back to bed. In between, he'd been in engineering, and he warned we'd need tickets and perspicacity to see the Alhambra when we'd meet up again, after Aaron's wedding, in Granada. He slept on his stomach. Tummy time. He often slept in jeans. The jeans changed, there was a flickering of outfits on his sleeping form and I wanted to know how.

He contacted Kristen years later, in Oakland, through OkCupid. I warned her, feeling hilarious, "Don't drive with him." Don't sleep and drive, man. Don't fuck him it's like fucking sleep the depressed the ghosts. Don't travel and only sleep in the fucking hostel. Pathetic. Don't study three things. He was upset, he said, when we did speak, about having studied film, about what is art education, which drove him to the arms of engineering, so heartless, he said, so now he wanted nursing. To help others at last.

So much sleep, it seemed like a big depression for Murat, like aloneness he didn't desire later confirmed by his presence online, his interest in Kristen who he did not know, he could not have known, knew.

Don't do it, Kristen. Don't date Murat, she didn't. You'd have to tell him. I saw what you did on your big trip around. Don't date a depressed person. He said he'd been to the Alhambra, had been perspicacious about ordering a ticket in advance, from Seville. We imagined him sleeping there, in the Islamic castle, on the tile. We were on an opposing, corresponding path. We only eclipsed for 30 minutes, while Kristen was in the hostel's shower. He went back to sleep, like excusing himself into Alhambran space, into improbable Arabic math, or I don't know, butcher murder. Whatever were your dreams, they kept changing, and you never saw her.

NIPPLE
Peeled claw, naked, eagle-shod. Just Dad.

DR. MONEY
We talked about Rilke who lived in Ronda briefly, sick of Paris, a writer of a monograph on the sculptor Rodin, who he liked so much for that immutable softness, the clothier of stone and marble, blood and soft life inside of stone, and marble.

A monograph on an artist like that is aggressive, and also shy, an embittered love letter—"You would never listen to me directly, would you, so I must, about my love for you, solicit the whole public. And you are a monster who would only love me through the conduit of *your* art, my reconnaissance of it, only there would you be so touched by me. I will even remove you from your art (as you want) so it shines with you in it and monstrous without you, what can lope centuries (if they are left) from your minor entrails, and it will never return to you like a dog a boomerang. I let your art lope. I *am* its loping."

Rodin kicked Rilke out of his life, because of such a crush, the monograph the crushing shyness. "He was supposed to be my secretary."

"I was more."

Dr. Money wrote to me still, years since Spain, when I was visiting Kristen again, in the middle of the night. I wrote back to him a description of myself, "Having become shrewd and routinized."

He did not write back not to my honest account of what has happened (the coquetry I exhibited on the plane diminished), how I had replaced my coquetry finally with depraved and competent artistry, Susanan.

I told him, "Like a mule."

SPECULUM

She came into Manuel's house, where the artists would live if they would ever arrive. I was there alone at that point, a prototype, at discount (I think). She broke the mirror like Plato breaks Luce

Irigaray's body: Irigaray (the second-wave feminist French psychoanalyst) retains her being, the stolen being of being a woman, stolen (from her) by the symbolic ordering, it is known. But she retains herself behind the mirror, this is the "nothingness that I am," woman who has to reflect man, but behind it she *is* there, crouching in the silver backs like old gorillas.

WHITE MATERIAL

I put my hand on the table. Everyone young was out of town into the Catholic procession, the processing night. It was my desk now. I claimed it like a dog with my palm. I pressed it into the wood, so boldly. My hand did not crouch to touch this table. I pressed it right in.

PUPPY

I biked to the convent in the morning past a young falabella and a receded mosque and cows their eyes like malted bells, or I walked as I liked with one of Manuel's little mugs like a smug American who likes to walk with a drink like that. The percolator was too tight. This was tea.

Abuelas and abuelos called, "Sit, sit," or "Come inside, come here," when they saw me like this, cup steam coming out like fume from a marsh in Duras.

At the convent, I read Ponge in the anteroom to starting anything else. I sat outside at a table in the far corner but all I can remember is the puppy put a fetal bird she'd pulled from a bird's uterus right onto this book where it lay open and had been held that way by a few stones pinned open like for surgery, on my little table, this bird was so fetal, man, a tan little bag of luminescing blood the puppy tore further into my book by Ponge. I can't remember the title.

The puppy bit the sac until this unmalfeasant and nascent bird was utterly flattened into the book. I can no longer be surprised that later she would have so very many fleas, all over hurting her. And these people. These hippies. They refused to even wash her with a little soap.

SANJAY

What I wanted was a word in. He talked so much. He said so much about street food and things at random like cruise ships like a lot of hostel conversations with young men—we were too old for this shit even then, in 2011, but we were and are poor, women writers, who work for things like online universities and tutoring portals and bakeries for years and years, so we were just there, man, soaking in the random fun with young men who like how random things are. Those cruise ships are craazy. We thought it was so random, so boring. But it turned out to be a major incident from his life. People died. It redeemed him.

QUINCE

We all went to a long lunch, the only kind. It was an elaborate spread in the country, just for us, a welcome from an established family who lived up in the country. This was a cultural immersion into Spain through the personal and elaborate history of a gracious and peaceful family, who were multigenerational on the hill. I remember especially quince. I sliced myself off a lot of quince aspic. After lunch and a lot of drink on the hot hill the sun like a rope, everyone except Bruno (who still drank) unwound from the long outdoor table and found their place to nap. In Spain you siesta where you are.

I walked around during the four-hour nap. I walked myself to the drained and small soaking pool cut into the hill like a blue intersection of a coffin the sun elaborating its old paint and I looked down at Aramingo and, with boredom and relief, looked and found the castle.

I walked back around and into the house. Even Bruno was asleep.

I had been writing at the convent. They had torn me from it. For this cultural immersion, and in Spain part of culture could be about sleeping together all sprung around the house and grounds now like from a narcotized can. I found all of them like that a murder scene stylized like a Haneke film, in each room, Susana snoozing on the couch in the salon, the abuelo in the chair across from her, Bruno at the table still, elegantly sleeping in his seat, Iván in the grass with his baby, asleep, and his wife I believed in a bed upstairs, perhaps she was delicate, Ángel on the porch sweetly slumped and the matriarch out of sight, the plates out, the quince aspic still available and so immobile in squares like marigold haikubes—I wanted you.

I couldn't sleep, I did not could not immerse. I walked around. I walked and looked. At nothing, nothing thrived. I walked to the drained pool and saw her there, sitting inside and looking out, awake too, American also though she had come here, pregnant, to start this life, and I only passed her like a ghost.

ÁNGEL

Ángel wouldn't look at the moon though it was shining and round and so still and pale. He wouldn't look up as we walked with Susana to the square for small beers in the quiet narrows.

I thought, Ángel, aren't you savoring this as I am? Who are

you and who am I? Don't we only want the walk? That large place is already dead. The walk could be alive, why don't you look?

The moon is a lot. Ángel, look.

Goddammit, look at it.

He kept his head down in the cobblestones, their parched bluffs. I wanted him to look at the shining stone. That country that can't come down. Eighth continent, breached. Like an eyeball isolated from everyone, the pupil painted white. But the shining moon is hollow as far as anyone could ever tell from earth. And I don't believe (like Kubrick knew) we've ever been.

ACID + FRENADOL

Because of the acid I had bad periods. I had them very hard, not excessive blood but tearing, shoe-burning, wicker knuckles creaking in the flexing and the cutting.

I didn't go anywhere for five days. I stayed in Manuel's room, floored with pain, man. I found a heating pad in a box from the 1970s. The photograph of the woman on the box was like a drawing of a woman made of a white nylon system. A heating pad works from the 1970s and it soothed my pain greatly, it kissed me with the hot truth of any time. The cheapest tweed was screaming to be ripped like a bandaid off the inside of my uterus, but the heating pad did something here.

In Spain I had such bad periods. I had a body full of pig's blood at that point, and bread, and tomatoes, and coffee. I bought coffee at the market. The percolator was too tight.

I looked at the castle from Manuel's bed. I let it hold me. I strapped myself to it looking at it and did not leave this earth, dying, from cramps. I clutched the heating pad to me. I folded it to apply great heat. The pharmacy was closed. I took some Frenadol in water. My companion. It blew the heating pad right out of the water. My spine was like a snake of vivacious valium. I traveled to the most blissful ground of being plastic and flexing with neutral to pleasure feelings. Frenadol is invisible in water like an angel indistinguishable in gender, in me dividing me for greater use of myself everywhere, my uterus departed like a bubble from my body like the moon hovering over us the shining hysterectomus. Frenadol obliviated my horrific cramps and I became energetic linguine in the night.

A PRICK

He only stayed for a week. It was over quickly, the siege of Manuel's house. The snoring and the use of my desk.

When he was leaving for New York he came into my room without knocking wondering if I had parts for his computer and

I indeed had a lot of leftover technology add-ons from my laptop failure at the start, from the order this town fruitfully overfilled for me (eventually). Aramingo was fruitful. I wrote here. It took not too much of my undeserved money. When you said hello to anybody the face would light at the recognition of a word: hello. You had to say it first, the guts. Otherwise, the face only passed you. A Scottish Spanish was spoken in this tiny town, you did not even say an "s" at the end of gracias. You said "hola" to anyone and could feel like a god turning a stone face woolen. And then you'd call goodbye, too, when the sweet abuela passed, and she'd call this back like loons. I learned nothing, and to disregard, with people, a first hard feeling. If you have the guts. I gave this prick the technology he required to go home, to reconvert his computer to New York. He already had his hands all over the pieces and wires on my shelf and was taking them anyway scooping the add-ons into his carrier. He said goodbye and took my picture, with Vera, to document he'd experienced us.

Adio, Prick.

SUSANA

I sat with Susana on the terrace at Manuel's. There were many places jutting from his house, where he died, where you could sit.

Susana lit candles and had something to drink. My balcony was above us. Everything exhausted me.

Susana talked about her sister's baby and a postpartum condition, in Spain in Catalan the "quaranta," where you bleed for forty days. I had not heard of this in Spain or English. A quaranta, it's too much, to be giving milk and losing blood, to be *such* a punctured bag. I'd die. To have a child when the world is dead like this, and to bleed an afterbirth for forty days, was Susana right? Do you know it, the quaranta? Do Americans have it?

Susana said she would not mind bleeding for this long. Capable, robust, and sojournal. Bruno had left in Chile something like four children. He was an old man. He seemed on the run, scurrilous, scurrying. He wanted to stay in Spain, and he hoped to marry my Susana to stay here. I didn't want it.

The quaranta, I had never heard of it, like a big secret. Susana's Secret. Woman to woman. You have to hear it. Internetless you have to find your Susanan terrace. You can't have one (a son or a daughter) and be finished. You have to then bleed for forty days to pledge your allegiance to loss while you nurse. Forty days of blood. Think of night. You can't have a kid, addiction in his blood like that. It would be so painful loving an addict. Addicted to milk, and life, and light.

XANAX

I went to the bathroom in the plane to wipe my mouth. I couldn't swallow after half a Xanax. I still can't (sometimes) when anxiety comes. Sometimes it comes back. There are whole swallowing clinics where people regain their strength, to take it.

I wiped up my mouth and returned to my seat, and the flight attendant came by and I can't tell you how tenderly told me, "Don't you know to read by light."

HENRY

He called my cell before I left Montana, in the week before the flight to Philly, from there to Spain. He said he was drunk and bottomed out and needing a burger, he was so devastated and hungry. Désespoir. After the burger, he went back out, leaving me in the place, the apartment I had really already left. I was staying with Anne Marie, Ben, sleeping on the floor beneath their Christmas tree like Jesus Christ.

He said, "I can drink so much more now that I'm full." He said, "So thanks."

I said, "Your coat."

IT WAS RAINING + VERA + SHEEP

I sat on the balcony reading Vera's monograph on the artist Robert Irwin, that artist of space and white and light. It was raining. I kept the loose pages in order like her sister.

Vera rolled wool at a desk at the convent. It was piling. She didn't have herself filmed or photographed, no one could know what happened. She didn't document her art, as Irwin, too, wouldn't allow photographs of certain walls that emitted or welcomed light at angles. A photo doesn't always help.

Vera made a pile of rollies of the filtered hair of sheep here. She'd washed it at first with the locals in a contained pool of stream water they'd cowed there. They cleaned and dried and rolled local wool into lines of bales I could see from my balcony. It was Manuel's. She hauled a bale to the convent that she depleted into fingers, cigarettes, neat, like a New Yorker rolling her joints, for no film. I couldn't believe it as I typed. On a laptop you see a monotone animé of your shameful will.

I don't know what it is, her art. She put wool all the fuck over it. These artists, her and Bob Irwin. Irwin doesn't even let a photograph in. You can't photograph the light on what he whitepaints on all walls like his monotonous existential discontiguous mural. Vera didn't make any record of what she did in Aramingo.

The moon the crescent moon like a tusk glued with spume to a mirror.

Vera relied on being recorded accidentally somehow. I somewhat watched her from where I was sitting, bored to be alive. I couldn't believe it. It would be hard to record anything, so boring. She warmed herself by the white fire, the consolation for living for life repeating, of sheep.

BRUNO

Bruno wanted to marry a Spaniard. He looked for a willing or broken or bored or enterprising or anyone. Susana reminded me of my mother, Taurus-y. She was finished with her boyfriend, the Swiss cow counter, and she needed a place to crouch for the coming year at least. She was crouching there. She didn't pay them. She managed Manuel's house in exchange for a room. She photographed me at the convent from a distance while I was at a table. There were only a few chairs. I have this picture of her standing there, taking me.

I don't know if she might have married Bruno. It was his plan. I don't know at all if she injected her sheepdogs with heroin and Xanax halves and bludgeoned them and said, "Ok, they are sleeping, come on in." The air pills with geometry, blocks. I can't find out on the internet what happened.

Vera and I paid our residency fees, for months in advance, draining the funds from our culminations, and these are the angry partings I can have with my cash. I unload myself, I fling it in the contracting bin in the air.

I don't know if Susana is still there in Aramingo like a bull.

VERA + SHEEP, SHEEP

Vera rolled paper actually, not the wool. I recall she did wash the wool. But she rolled the papers, empty cigarettes piling up. She would show the pile in a gallery later, in New York, she carried the papers out of Spain like a spy, like from Russia, she was Russian but no one could have known what it was her sitting there so quiet like a bull of fortitude in the face of draining funds, making empty rollies. She was Russian American. I went up the hill with her and we saw sheep together. They didn't want us to go in any manner, they were having small beers in the square before their big coordinated nap. They said, "Sleep, sleep." We might as well have taken a rocket or decapitated Spain to have biked up the farm hill at naptime, these sheep in so acute their circles, this land of moons in the awful sun, all full.

Paper is nothing, no place, Utopia: what that word actually means. You can't go inside of paper: you aren't here. Vera rolled papers: you smash flat Utopias into the tunnels out of there.

HENRY

I wrote Henry letters. I wrote to him real mail on Manuel's old stationery from the '50s very frail, the paper would disintegrate in anyone's mouth. Everyone is wet.

I wrote: In silence, in pure moment, you visit. The rain, the chair, the clear evening's rip of pink, the color honking even and simmering then (a dispersing bell of plangent-pinkness over the darkness of evening ending) over the mountain, a calm, healthy heart, the feel of the most calm and quiet exuberance—these things.

I wrote: I love to think about a gentle-boiled egg in your hands for me.

I wrote: I have not seen you in a very long time. It is funny to think about seeing your face in motion. Your eyes gulping and smothering my face.

I would have addressed them into the bathroom, back to Christmas. It was spring. If I could, into him like wrapping a heart in a letter in disintegrating butcher paper sent. I sent these papers most geriatric desiccate anorexic most emaciated first aid—thinnest, tri-folded bandage, as if there were the wound, the opening. I opened: "Dearest one." Superlative as if there were for me other options.

I AXED THE PIG HEAD

Ornamented courtyard, firepit and light-strung. Standing around at night. English so scarce, there is Spanish, of course, and even a little French—two Lyon-living daughters of a man from here. They visited home fully pursed with French bags and intelligent. They spoke Spanish and French and some English. I axed the pig head, otherwise, I couldn't talk much. This was a ready-made Spanish sentence I could just dash off, the long dash down the pink head, you have to drop the axe and press the dash into the cavity the anteroom of aromatic meat.

I couldn't learn Spanish. I said certain sentences, I forget everything. The Americans who spoke Spanish wouldn't cross back, to English. They were there, here, in Spain. It was right. I wanted to leave (always) immediately. The courtyard confined, the lights that were strung were pinpointing the prison, the conversations. Only the Prick convinced people, when he arrived, to speak in English or to sit back, bemused and spacing. But I left. I wanted to go home to Manuel's house and use my desk, to spend my time with English. In Spain, there was Spanish and sometimes French inside courtyards, my happiness all this English all mine, in my powers, will, and shame.

SANJAY

Kristen photographed us, timing the camera, her Chinese pink parasol hovering ever quivering above her like the exalted pink rectum of a vulture, crepe and bright. Following. It made men follow us wherever. They called, "Blonde." Like Monica Vitti or Madonna or a blonde woman.

She photographed us together exalting in our physical difference. I am smaller, browner, and in black.

In the hostel in Cordoba, for Aaron's wedding, a young Italian (a man) slipped papers under our door, wanting to meet her. He pursued her, poured notes inside of our room. He pursues her now, online. There were women from Britain in the hallway most of the time on their drawing holiday. They drew together in their sixties, seventies. Kristen looked around for the pursuit of an Italian while we spoke to them, about painting.

She is so appealing.

Sanjay approached on the roof, he said, "May I sit here with you?" and I thought, Come on, oh, man, again. I waited for what male interruptus. They interrupt us. They were always after her. Her shocked baby look and that hair like the insides of apples in color, soft spaghettini of feather, feather.

But Sanjay didn't pursue Kristen. I seemed to be there. He made eye contact, at least, with us both. He recounted seeing everyone including his family and friends out there in the ocean in the tiny boats in the blue ocean with night's embers glowing off the blue, gray, pigeon vinegar uproaring. The moon making it all rough. It was crazy, nuts. He spoke to us both. We were on the roof. We sat together at the table he'd joined politely.

He'd asked.

It was so serious. Night fell on the small boats.

The sun set underneath our roof. "There were, like, oars, man."

Night billowed in buildings from a gold line. Chalk thick.

I tried to control the situation like it was a bad one like *The Shining*, a bad situation at a hotel, now that it was dark and the moon was escalating and upscaling, and the sun was exshining having excreted all of its exrising.

ÁNGEL

I told Ángel about a friend I'd lost—insignificant. I had freaked out then, though, to have been cut off like that in the newt part of the twenties, you think friendship is a solid moving state. It will move me through life. I didn't think: It doesn't.

I dreamed of her every night for a year or two. There, there, and there you are. I couldn't control the visits, I told Ángel, and sometimes they didn't hurt. My mind was still bewildered she was gone and I must have been in love. I must have wanted her, like sex, and I remember: gripping each other in order to look (at all, up) at the moon.

I dreamed of her continuously, I do now. I know myself the self, I know I'll dream the thing tonight to have written to have rubbed the perfuming bag of her in my bowel, the auburn, glasses, the short hair, the shorn one, I shaved you in my room, the green pants, black velvet jacket are you kidding, the white sweater she had what was it the sheep, the velvet fetid sheep of chemically velvitized wool, your breasts what the fuck like Gaelic boulders in water coming out in so much fog and distance.

I dreamed and dream, I told Ángel that night, his haikubes about on the dining table, being insignificant, the random sentence work. Your graying black hair, suit sometimes like you're a ghost.

I told Ángel I was tortured by this friend's disappearance. It was over. She went away, man. She discontinued what I did, I had I think swiped a caress at her. Jesus. I sent Ángel what I wrote once, about this night in Aramingo when we had shared our despairs, his writing teacher taking his girlfriend like that and when I told him about her (I emailed him from Salt Lake), but I'd changed the arrangement. I warned him in a preface to the attachment. I wrote that we had danced in the salon to a record of Manuel's, *La vie en rose*. I wrote Susana out, man. I smashed her into him. It simplified the narrative. It was raining. It was.

LIGHT OF OTHER DAYS

I watched an Argentine film in Philadelphia, in 2005, with my rich ex, in a movie theater and for free. I made my love into a bough above the cash, from which to swing to love him freely: he decided what we did.

We were seeing this film. In it, a daughter is the administrator, she has to, of her famous father's estate. Dead poet like Borges, a writer. Famous like that, a foundation wants all of his diaries. She reads them, to check. *What did he think of me?*

He thought she had not been worth having.

She tears out the sheet that says it and hides it on her thigh, up her skirt, as the foundation comes calling. They know she is a snake, a bourgeois woman, and is capable of holding it all back like Foucault's family, like Joyce's family. Sade's family. Difficult bearers of estates. When she finally hands over his diary and the foundation leaves with it, she peels this stolen page from her thigh and her skin has broken out. Like a sheep dipped in blood, it's a very red rash.

I wrote to Samuel about the email from *Light of Other Days*, that shamed us like that to have written those bad love letters to each other. The commission was totally off. I was so ashamed, so reddened.

They wrote: *i hope the america you found can be worth something for you. we were hoping to find the way to india instead and cant really figure out of what to do with new land you set foot on.*

I could not work with this bad email, push it press it anywhere on me at all. I could not make it topical. Though I was so ashamed to have failed these fake Swiss photographers, how I wished they were a couple of fakes. We were real. Maybe our love was real. But their book without us is actually available, with an included short story by Stanislaw Lem.

NIPPLE

My father touched my nipple.

My right nipple turned red for a week, before the flight to Spain. It is usually very brown.

I removed him, his finger from my nipple, right out on the street. His girlfriend was behind him. I had no one behind me. My right nipple turned red for a reason. Because it loves me.

IT WAS RAINING

Emma lives with her father before she leaves that home, their farm. Beautiful peacocks and shit mill around in the same sentence, the same pen. In *Madame Bovary*.

"Right along the outbuildings extended a large dunghill, from which manure liquid oozed, while amidst fowls and turkeys, five or six peacocks, a luxury in Chauchois farmyards, were foraging on the top of it."

Flaubert kills Emma, the wife, he deadens the wife concept. There was no WiFi conceptually in the whole of Manuel's when it rained, or the town, at all, so I read, and wept to be there, here, when I wouldn't have gone there.

BUS

I wanted to leave Aramingo *badly*. I had had a poor time. I had outcasted myself but there was anger at this place. The fleas. The fleas they still said to me were mosquitos. The conspiracy was alive. My paranoia about many things won't ever deteriorate. Iván took me to the doctor, his uncle. His uncle said, "Flea bites, sure." Claro is a word. He was the only rational person like Jesus Christ. The broken house. My ailments and the out internet, and the processions the parties, explosive. The disruption of the quietude of all roses, *frequently*.

The amplifiers were set up by the stream and blared digital salsa one afternoon, a salsa that had been derived, ingeniously, from the derivation of a cell phone ring—the cell phone ring from 2001 phones started to salsify itself, started to stomp, the ring, in belled boots, to dance salsa, and this is what blared on a loop, by the stream, and the castle is stale and popping like popcorn with vermin, and the puppy—sweet bitten pup—I had to cross her entirely off of my heart.

They had wanted me to work with them on the delineation, the soil leavening and design, of their labyrinth up there at the convent, a mile or so from Manuel's in town, and to help plant some potatoes into a parched plot like a harshly smashed boulder, iridescent tan. Gestures for pics, worker-artists with shovels, they were building a global artist residency like building a website. There were very few chairs, lights, plugs. I found some sun, on a break from writing what, somewhere along the bobo potato farm. You go along. The Spanish sun fulfilled me like coffee, what constancy of pure copper caked like that in burning butters. Metallurgical, the air is mineral wheel pulling me.

Things were wrong there. There was anger everywhere there, a colony of anger.

I waited for the bus I wanted so badly but in the wrong place. I waited where the sign was (for it) for a time until an abuelo said where the bus was (over there, just behind). I had no cash. The ATMs in Aramingo were husks. This place, the edifices cycling in white walls very low, contiguous, its holidays the most acute thing. Poor town for global art, for working on what. Holidays smash art obfuscate it. Ruin life-forms. They burn books. Fireworks attack books.

The bus has a credit card slot. It's glorious.

BREAST

She took her breast out into the white air of the convent. Her daughter was in Bruno's arms (her daughter's grandfather) like a Renoir. He was Chilean, and corrupt, with a jolly belly. I wanted to claw him from Susana. He wanted Susana, her citizenry like a perfume that turned him (the old man) to her very breast. The breast of Spain. Spain was collapsing in 2011 and would collapse imminently almost all the way, economically, from the insides like treason but the reasons are quite American. But he wanted her—it, Spain. It, her. No work for anyone. Would Bruno pay her? Would it ensure her a room there?

He moved his granddaughter to the breast of his daughter. He airplaned her to it, cute. His daughter had not seen him for a long time. He'd shown up in Spain. He'd had quite a few other, younger children. He hadn't had her in Chile very often. She grew with her mother, New Yorker, American. Now he was here being so jolly. Showing up at times to Manuel's, to say hello to Susana. Making jokes. Seeing to it.

Susana suggested we get some ice cream together, it would be nice if we did that, us two. She pointed as we walked to a dust-bitten sign for this, ice cream. We didn't do such a thing. She photographed the castle in the dark. A long exposure of it. She only exposed herself to making it. She went out, alone, of course. I sat with the ants and looked at them, the sun stuffing their skin cherry vermillions. The sun overdosed kale so nutritious the green like black kelp. This was friendship, I think, more than an ice cream outing, it's a true friend thing: you don't do a thing.

I hated Bruno. He was wiling time waiting for Susana's desperation to come onto him. He airplaned his granddaughter to his daughter's breast where she sat boyish, but with a truly large breast, full of Hélène Cixous's white ink, but I'm the writer, and he did it unlike a warplane kamikaze pilot, insignificant, distracted by his personal schemes about Susana, divested in the aim, the target (his daughter's nipple).

SHEEP

Vera and I went away from Spain in the afternoon, anti-nap. Everyone's mass nap cleared Spain from its own farms, olive trees, clarified for us a quite American afternoon. Spain got into all the beds (to keep cool) in Spain on marble floors. We biked like American ribbons whipping the afternoon's hot end.

It was so hot that I fainted.

That evening I finally just smoked some fucking hash. I had barely had a drink in that Spain, a sobriety my emblem to alcoholism. Though Frenadol did make sprite and hopeful my spirit! I finally smoked hash *at last*. People I did not like I liked them. I spoke to Vera and the man who was pursuing her that evening, on the balcony off the salon. The moon was saranwrapped in moonfilm like sateen, and I looked up at the full castle—stoned, nothing shames. That castle, there like an elephant indignant and out of Africa, on the Spainhill. Hash sweeter and stickier like the pussy the dried fruit the cum-twat of marijuana.

I touched the balcony stone (black) and spoke to Vera about art her Fulbright, back to Russia, and my heart filled lucid with the black stone of the balcony where swims inside Manuel's both hands, mothy in the hardness.

MURAT

During the single half hour Murat was awake he recommended to us (Kristen in the shower) an Argentinian place in Málaga. We ate plates of mauve beef there and the acid came for me. We walked through a tunnel trying for farmacia. There was one, we had heard, with a late-nite counter. People were lined up on the street. I felt incredibly beeflogged. The Spanish Tums came into my system, on a bench. We could not walk, I could not. I waited impatiently to feel like nothing again in Spain like nothing. When we returned Murat was sleeping.

Claro.

ARAMINGO

There were very few chairs at the convent, very few lights to work underneath of. Friends came, smoked and were talking about bluer-collar callings. Farmings. Collard greens. Groups of friendly men clumped on and around the few chairs, artists standing around in corners or being drawn to small beers and invitations out, elsewhere. But artists steal. They steal the truth and pump it with venoms and toxins and perfumes. They have actually the deepest of incuriosities in the world and the darkest hatred for groups, and for groups of men. Her friendship, if you've found a friend in her, is a crude skiff that she tries to offer as a salve (of some color) over the numb water. I filled a marigold little skiff with candles but they masturbated until they were dead, and I was really done socializing. I really was. I could not go on smiling at them, at situation. There is no artist's situation. There is no country that makes me come. I was really in Spain for no reason.

WEDDING

She was crying. She said she'd been depressed. I thought about medication. Kristen thought (she was thinking about her brother) not that.

SPECULUM

She was warm and generous in her expressions like Kabuki theater. Extended frozen gesture. She was unfruitful to talk with. She said she was sick of Americans and their want for the internet, and their want of options. Hot water in the shower. The internet is like a grave expansion a grave expanding. She was sick of people coming to Spain and wanting to be like young, unattached American women. She was referring to me. "This is country living," she said at the bar in a jumpsuit she had bought from a country shop full of things from Asian factories like Taiwan, Bangladesh, looking hip and warm, her gestures protracted and glazed in an extension of beatitude that befell and bell-stretched her manner but was not her. She broke that fucking mirror. She looked well, beautiful, and natural, and smoked regretfully after nursing, in sweet, neurotic moderation. The Prick was her old and good friend. He had come to support the endeavor because he was anyway in Spain. He made for us a meal, for Vera, me, Susana, an extensive feast of Spanish highlights at Manuel's. Just for us girls. Susana took hers into her room, sick with menstruation. It wasn't a poor time. No one ever sat for dinner at Manuel's. It was before his girlfriend arrived. And she, his good friend, had in fact gone. She had taken Vera's money, for three months up front, derived from the power and the promise and the pictures on the website, from theater this sham, and she was gone with it her ticket her kid on a plane to New York.

SUSANA

Susana ate bread without a way, not a tradition, manner or even a rough manner. It was always different, she only ate hungrily, however the hunger dictated her to eat, but had her salad after meat like dessert. She increasingly cooked for Bruno. He was over at Manuel's. On my balcony, I had coffee with a salamander. Its verdancy was lime. I bought Thai cooking sauce in the store so random, the red candy pussy of hardly spiced cherry honey. I glooped it on kale that had grown here and had black kelp inlaid in its green. There were so many farms all around Aramingo. Fresh vegetation. Vera too liked to eat alone, standing. In a suit in the doorway, standing once, Manuel.

WEDDING

She said she had paid to go to an artist's colony, too, through her tears about a depression she had been in, at Aaron's wedding in Cordoba. She said it was in a rotting farmhouse in Belgium. She said she had walked in a veil through the woods for a video artist, who had been her roommate in a rotten room, and they went generally unfed and without blankets or respect. She said a squalid couple who had nothing were consigned to them, the artists. The couple managed them. She said there must be a video somewhere of her walking through the woods in a veil as there are photographs of this person in the butcher's freezer of Aramingo, in a silk slip its nipples like a panic of stallion marbles.

A *piteousness* of doves, so a panic of nipples.

WEDDING + ACID + FRENADOL

I had acid, big pain, my gut was like a knife aquarium again. But it changed when I left that town and I was safer with my Kristen a reason for life, it transmuted acid problems mostly into a bad cold I developed at Aaron's wedding. I coughed blood in the toilet at the wedding at the beach and I told Lauren, in the night, "It's TB," but it was the groom's cherry salsa from Michigan, conglomerated in the throat in the evening. Now I had a very bad cold. I took Frenadol my friend jamming its big packets into small teas at any tapas. I was losing my voice. I coughed on the plane all through my almost voiceless conversation with Dr. Money. He warned me: "You don't have conversations like this all of the time. In grad school for a few years, yes, everyone's so interested, but after that, you won't have this again. You don't know."

He warned me this was actually love we were having. But, I considered that I had read to him on the plane *L'espace littéraire*, from Maurice Blanchot, and that is just, nice. *L'espace littéraire* dans l'avon, c'est bon, c'est tout.

Ce n'est pas anything else.

I was out of Frenadol in the US and in the American west where Henry flew in. We met up in Salt Lake City. I stopped coughing in his arms. I stopped ejecting violently loogies, green balzacs of black bat hearts. Henry stopped that. It's not only the only sex in the world but my throat relaxing at last my voice relaxing perhaps this on the surf of sleeping on you.

I wrote to Dr. Money from my new apartment (in SLC) about a pattern of diamonds on the wall above the bed from some of the old stained glass in the brick house, so recently the former flop house, the mortar roach vase.

I have a stained glass window in my bedroom so at night, the wall fills with diamonds, I wrote.

My neighbor called his cat, Lucy, "my daughter." He did molest her asshole.

ARAMINGO

In Aramingo, people walk right into your house, into the middle of the salon, an old pueblo custom. Abuelas are tottering in, people who were remembering Manuel. I greeted them as the new Manuel, his classical records a bit broken and still being played like a shivering horse's knee being fried in circles on the dining table (what I'd hoped to break like a horse into my desk).

"Welcome," I said.

I offered an abuela some coffee. It was before Susana had arrived, ruining the percolator with her justified anger I'm sure. I should be so sure about the anger of women anywhere. You can break the mirror, man. I'm sure.

Nobody wanted anything but to look all around as much as they could, these abuelas almost daily in the beginning, when I was there alone. They hadn't been inside before, these old women. They came so often, while I was writing. They didn't know Manuel, who was alone in Spain, too, I'm positive, alone in Aramingo, who hadn't invited them over ever and maybe was a homosexual the Francophile, his recordings of young men of the French revolution speaking poems onto the street's microphonic tongue, and you do not walk into the house of a man even in this situation where you do these little things in Aramingo, Spain. Customs about entry pertain to women only. Man is the universe. Literature is written on speeding sheets of space.

SHEEP

A thought knocked me over, it made me faint. My whole heart hurled like a red boulder past my ears into Spain, up the hill biking. My heart was beating. When we stopped biking, the bikes broken, I could hear it had gotten like raccoons into everything. The clouds. Shit. I fainted pretty badly by the road, on a tree, and Vera in a panic, she thought I was so sick. I'm not that sick. I told Vera I was fine. This happens. Fainting does. She didn't understand. She wanted us to return, to go back down there. I hated that, the square and their small beers, their discouragement of us being out like this in the heat, even in our youth like this, and their youth, was it enough to kill us? they had wondered out loud in the square, their beers so small, so no, I would not return to Spain yet, I had to show Vera how young and strong I am, the living, anyone alive is so very young, and I rode with strength past her capable biking, because really we needed to run as fast as possible from that small square up here to find only the best, the circles of heaven. The sheep (in their want of shade) made that very possible.

NIPPLE

I told my mother what happened. I reported the incident. And I called my rich ex. He said, "Tell the world, darling! Tell the whole world!" I was in his loft, him in Boston. I assured him, "I am vacuuming." My life was everywhere in there still, cups and books and postcards, little notes, boxes of stuff like glitter that gets places. Like Kristen's hair appearing for a year more after she sublet our apartment for one month (in Montana). I found the strands, inestimably long, and I would boil with thoughts of Henry cheating on me with somebody blonde and then remember, "It's ok, it's another of K's. She lived here. Kristen lived here for one month." These strands would surface and swim into vision at opportune times.

Henry said, "I can drink so much more now that I'm full." He said, "So thanks." And I saw a strand somewhere of her hair like a whale.

I said, "Your coat."

My mother said, "I believe he did touch your nipple. He'd do that." She said, "He was always inappropriate." Like Jack Nicholson chasing his own son in *The Shining* through a labyrinth at the hotel, with his axe, the mother Shelley Duvall in the bathroom, trapped, who could not protect him like she can't even walk anymore or move from the bed any longer.

I called Henry. I told him what had happened. I told him my own father had touched my own nipple right on the street the labyrinth, first thing. I hadn't seen him in so long. We hadn't really spoken since he'd been in that bathroom.

KAREN

Karen said I could live in her house while she was out of town, the week before my flight. So I left Anne Marie and Ben's.

I moved into Brandon's mom's, a real house. A bedroom, a bed. But I was not allowed to say where I was. Her condition, and to keep things very clean. There were instructions about this, and vacuums. I should scour my leavings.

I was humiliated having to behave like this (an abused woman). Like this was a safe house. I wasn't abused I was forgotten. Drugs displaced me from Henry's considerations and he slept in our bed with an old friend, c'est tout.

Hobo spiders had come in through our window near this bed, and they have such toxins. Everyone in Montana knows: "Avoid Hobos." They will maim your nervous system. I trapped them while Henry worked and when he came back past midnight, he killed them revealing their guts like tawny balzacs. He killed one with a textbook, something misdelivered by Amazon and he'd opened the package anyway right away with the wrong name right there and kept the book on something scientific, I forget. And now this. A use. He dropped it down. The bomb. There was no morality in our family.

And he punched me once, in our sleep.

I wondered at Karen's (Brandon's mom's) what if a Hobo spider came in and bit them while they are on drugs (him and his friend). They won't notice enough to go to the emergency room to reverse the toxin. Everyone knows you have to go there, if you are Montanan, and you get bitten. They'll allow the fatal toxins, I thought, to maim them. I was concerned about them.

At Karen's I waited on a flight to Philadelphia I'd arranged before Christmas, for after New Years, to celebrate with a surprise party my mother's retirement. Thirty-five years at CLS, Community Legal Services. Her good work. I had my books shipped ahead to my dad's, the only garage I could think of. My mother's tiny place in the city her equipment in her closets. I asked him. I wrote an email. I hadn't spoken to him in a long time. I thought: "He can do this for me. My vulnerability opens me to this possibility." I thought: "This is the lesson."

Bildungsroman, you're not nice.

Abuse wasn't my problem. If Henry knew where I was (in Karen's immaculate house the artist's house) he'd show up drunk and we'd have sex, we'd fuck and break her art, and the freestanding glass cabinet. A crumb would catch on fire like daffodils everywhere, in all of the rooms, on fire. It wasn't the abuse, it was the turn on. The only sex in the world circling what the safe house like a jaguar, or ridiculous, a blustery turkey coming to get me the red wattle bubbling and wagging. Sex, the convincer. You goose. You gray dove after. He called me, he asked, "Where are you, my friend?"

Karen's art: She had written out the diary she had kept of her marriage (to Brandon's dad) onto her actual wedding dress, and photographed this. It's the photographs you see in the galleries, of a precise, elegant pen, a near-calligraphy on clothing, of things despairing or surprising enough.

I didn't tell.

He called my phone, sobbing. I don't know where he was. Off the rails and lost in a countryside with no inns.

He said, in a message, fumeful with cocaine and OxyContin, vodka, a history with methamphetamine, "I will learn."

I called Kristen. She was driving down California. We laughed that he would die.

I skyped with Aaron.

Nobody said, "Fuck him." We all laughed (so much) at how the moon swings into the white rifle of death, pointing what its whole barrel.

I left Montana. I sold my car.

NIPPLE

I had to have that brunch. I wanted my books.

IT WASN'T RAINING

I like to feel the sun on the back of my shirt or whatever I'm wearing like a man's thumb. "The sun is masculine" is a thing. Moon, you're over there, you're a woman. But the sun too is a woman who cuts off male thumbs, like club fingers. They feel so good, cut off like that, on my back when I'm quiet.

I sat around and looked down at the ants. I didn't look at the potato farming project or the labyrinth they were still building to spotlight on their website. I tried to look kind but you can't look kind and think at all.

I think the sun is a woman. I think interruptions disembowel her.

IT WAS RAINING

Emma moves in her marriage to a small town, to Yonville (like Dogville) that is as long as the shot of a rifle, and it ends in a cemetery at the end, on the way out of town.

Everyone knows each other and there is a famous fair at which is sold, so it's called out, "liquid manure."

"There is nothing more to see in Yonville. The street (the only one), the length of a rifle shot and lined by a few shops, ends abruptly where the road bends. If you leave it on your right and follow the base of Saint-Jean hill, you soon reach the cemetery."

This is where she lives though she longs for Paris and other men than Bovary, her husband (the doctor), she is longing for a kind of romance she's read about in books and, like Flaubert did, she longs for the Orient.

She loves language, and wants the letters of her lovers, and amasses some letters (like the ones I had written to Emma) which her husband finds after she dies. (My friend, the one who cut things off now a decade ago, she was named Emma.) She kills herself. He finds out she didn't love him much. He sees that she had lived, under his nose right in Yonville, a life full of letters. He puts them on his skin and burns himself.

I wrote Emma letters all through her college. Where are they now, in a petrified Barnard dumpster?

As a cadaver Emma Bovary vomits some kind of black liquid. Is it a toss of dark water, an ejected phial from Ophelia's drowning area? She vomits black liquid, what is it? Flaubert didn't say, he doesn't write everything down, man. It's obvious if you aren't an idiot that she vomits black liquid shit.

IT WAS RAINING

They had to lift her head a little, and at that a stream of black liquid ran out of her mouth like vomit.

It's a void, liquefied. Emma is nothing. It's outer space, lique-fied and summoned, the proof she has no organs. It's the vomiting pen. It's that she's nothing is paper, but she's blushing. She acts like skin, seeming organ-y. What is this vomit? What kind? It's a sopping balsamic vinegar of her black heart, pressed. It's the black coffee I so badly needed as I read, the percolator tight.

KRISTEN

In Seville we went, at Murat's suggestion (in Málaga) in the half hour I talked with him, to Los Coloniales. It was a crowded restau-rant and you had to wait. In a beautiful courtyard. When we were seated I was overcome with hunger and emotion at being chosen and ordered duck liver. A whole lemon banged like a tomb on my skull from a tree, the instant I made an unsavory comment about a woman in front of us in the queue, to eat.

God punished me for what I said and then had to endure our laughter at how instant. Kristen still laughs at it. Good lemon. That was such a good punishment.

The waiter was infatuated with my friend and would not leave us alone, he asked for our names, to make conversation, to attach to us further. But he could not hear them, American names. We said them several times. He called after us with what he had heard, wanting her, saying goodbye, anything. But he'd heard it all wrong.

On the walk back to our hostel, "Carole" and "Constance" got lost in the old swirling streets (it was raining) of Seville and an old man led Kristen (I straggled behind, came with) to a dance place where he wanted to dance with her, and he promised her that this was actually in fact our hostel. Our hostel smashed into the dancing he wanted with her. He held onto her back, pushing her. I followed this. Before the dance, we ran. Into the rain. We found the hostel I don't know how they did it, that Constance, and her Carole.

VERA

Vera asked if I'd go on a date with her, because she wasn't interested in this person who'd asked her. I'd be a third wheel. He worked at the Prado in Madrid. He visited his mother in Aramingo often. He was in pursuit of Vera. He believed she would be his. He took us into the basement of a restaurant one pueblo over and on a Mac computer showed us a presentation about his family. It was a multimedia family tree which turned from photographs into paintings. Portraits of kings.

"Look," he said, "I came from kings."

He kept saying it, like it was a miracle. "I actually came from kings."

The presentation lasted for a long time, the restaurant even the basement of the restaurant, was closing, because he came from many, so many kings, on all sides.

He performed graphic design for the Prado and he showed us some postcards he had designed for that famous museum. It was, in truth, the only thing he had going for him, and it wasn't enough. The restaurant was closing but he made an agreement among men to keep the place open to keep showing these women a presentation. The chairs were going up around us like a fortress and he kept showing us the kings, the accordion on the screen of sliding paintings, so very common. It's common to paint men. Look in the offices of buildings.

"Can you believe it? I came from them. From kings."

This person's Mac died and there was nothing you could do for that here. It was done. He drove us home to Aramingo, probably muttering, "I came from kings." Whatever. He tried to keep Vera in the car, to drop me off. I took her the witch, like an evil wheel, the kink in the fate. I bludgeoned a royal tree and ate its king-plums, with my rectum. Fuck him. I took her with much laughter. "Come on. Out of the car!"

Vera was in love with someone in New Jersey. She skyped with that person when the internet bathed Manuel's house in the shining for an hour it seemed by accident spontaneous in an afternoon. She had to sit in the hall to talk with him. I saw her laughing.

It is not funny at all: "I came from kings."

I was so bored in Spain, bored in the basement with his presentation. I'm bored all the time, by men. I actually come from boredom.

JEAN-PAUL + JEAN-PHILLIPE

In the bookstore in Philadelphia, Jean-Paul bought me *Self-Portrait Abroad,* in translation. He said, "It might help." He did not know it.

It helps to be bought something right in front of you like that. Sunday boldness.

Women are humiliated in this little book (a travelogue) but the narrator, a character like its author (the author, Jean-Phillipe Toussaint), protects in his esteem and in his writing: his wife and also a little daughter. They are well taken care of. He exalts and treats as equals these particular females.

I had a professor in school who told us all the time like a siege on education: "My wife is hot."

No one said she wasn't, man. We hadn't seen her. I mean, he was our professor. He kept saying it like that, like "Fuck you *fuck you* my wife is hot." It was like a trump, "My wife is hot," he kept saying it to us angrily keeping his wife as "wife," keeping her appearance (like what is she, blonde, man? Is she Jessica Rabbit Hannah Arendt, what?) in our class, alive at any moment, the threat of who we weren't being and never would be, married to him and hot hot hot hot, coming down on us all the time, the heat, like a US bomb in this American writing program, where we were writing what, coming-of-age curios? No one knew what she did for money. I felt worthless (there).

Toussaint reveres his wife and daughter. Besides his wife and little daughter, women all over this deranged little travelogue, *Self-Portrait Abroad*, by this Belgian like King Leopold are treated so roughly in his rough little book, clearly. They are so fucking clear: It's clear what they're for.

He attends a writers' conference, for instance, and in attendance: four generations of Vietnamese writers and internationals like him and Tahar Ben Jelloun. No women. Olivier Rolin and Tahar Ben Jelloun . . . a row of Vietnamese writers in grayish short-sleeved shirts . . . pale, bald, and fragile . . . was a writer . . . The General Secretary of the Writers' Union . . . a small and trembling interpreter in a short-sleeved grayish shirt who translated his words . . . Once he had finished it was time for a representative . . . he read right to the end . . . from the cultural counselor . . . the head of the book office . . . the head . . . the person opened the little note between his fingers.

Him, his, he. It's not anywhere announced there are no women involved in international cultural meetings, in writing, no, it's not said, but the pronouns fumigate the pages of pussy energy. But women then come, even in this despicable little book. Two young women in fact appear in the writer's room, distractingly silent and discrete, who with a furtive swishing of their silk tunics start to clear away the teacups the men have been given, replacing them with cans of soft drinks and Tiger, the Singaporean beer (although it was just after nine in the morning), before bringing them soup bowls, salads and spring rolls, cold meats, rice, and raw vegetables.

There they are. There they go.

And Toussaint spots Jane Birkin.

She is asked in his book to sing a song to the conference something from her repertoire. She doesn't need this shit. She declines. She says no. The men insist: No, no, really, repeated Jane Birkin, who continued laughing and smiling.

Four generations of Vietnamese writers, those who'd fought against the French, those who'd fought the Americans, everyone in the big meeting room was clapping their hands and chanting: *a song! a song!*

We all chanted around the large U-shaped conference table.

Toussaint has her laughing like that. You can make anyone do anything, in writing. *Laughing and smiling.*

Jane Birkin couldn't refuse any longer, you can't resist four generations of Vietnamese writers.

No, you really can't. She sings a song. And he has her sing:

Et quand tu as plongé dans la lagune. Nous étions tous deux tous nus.

Duras will end you, Toussaint, in my writing. And, seriously, man, "I will love you until I'm dead."

SHEEP

Vera wanted to get off the bikes and walk, fearful about the sheep-dogs big and white, two of them bounding on either side in the fields, right and left, as we ourselves took the road. Dusk was putting berets on all the trees, voilà. Things were darkening. The dogs were loping. They were, to me, only bounding out a boundary. But Vera felt they would attack us. She requested we get off of our bikes and gesture down the hill only as bipedals. A peace offering. Innocence. We are not like wolves, or lions. As if we are good. Not Americans. She was stiffened and careful with fear. She walked her wheels. And insisted. I walked mine down.

But I didn't think the dogs thought of us. We were in different films. Nothing could touch us. We were only the shellacked oil rolling down a hill, impenetrable like that in a sea of numbing night.

But then the sheepdogs did join each other from either side of the road, the two from each field, right and left, and gathered the four of them the horsemen, and now bounding at us. We mounted energetically our bikes (because I'm fine) because really, we had to run.

COMMUNITY ACUPUNCTURE + HENRY

I tried to cure my arm in Philadelphia before I left for Spain. In Spain, I'd have to handle and carry my things. They said, Iván emailed, I'd be biking a lot to the convent where global artists would work and walk a labyrinth on breaks from the work, the art. I'd live in town (in the house of a dead communist who loved artists). I'd bike up the hill, have a desk and a breakfast. I would, if I wanted, learn Spanish. I was going so soon, so dutifully I tried to heal my fucked-up left arm.

The acupuncturist designed her needles around the ridge of my swollen tendon. She put a needle into the back of my head. "I can tell you've had this for a while."

The needles do not anesthetize like a mainlining. They are ferromagnetic steel. A human body is more metal than water, it's more mineral. The acupuncture needle opens its eyes in your arm, its eyes are open and casting under the human water and there see the rails of a metropolis of many minerals.

Remagnetization. Reimagining metal medicine. Freeing the metal bogs in you. Clarify the bogs. Draw the bogs toward speeding.

My arm felt better when I did this community acupuncture. It felt good like that to be quiet in a room with the other Philadelphians like a Quaker meeting from the times of Ben Franklin (on leather recliners though in hippy West Philly). The little red dots on my arm, after.

Like AA: those are rooms of these people, strangers like this who heal and off the rails of the American hospital system just in a room together, a circle of sheep. Their hot afternoon meeting in

Spain. At the rec center in Missoula, Montana, there was one every single afternoon. Henry refused most of them. He read Heidegger and Beckett. *Watt.* Because no one wants to be like them. "Sheep will never make insurrections," said Benjamin Franklin. He didn't get any better. He drank and inhaled cocaine and did OxyContin years after I left him, went to Spain, and when I returned. I was with him. Because he wanted a different cure. But you have to become (like Christ, his holes) so female.

SANJAY

We didn't even want the hostel special. Who wants to stay at the hostel for your dinner? You want to be among the restaurants, parks, and the people of Seville but we were hungry and had been followed by a man from store to store for the last hour. Where we went, a store (for gum, because of him), he did follow. It was daylight, just like that. People everywhere. They are.

Sanjay spoke for a long time like Marlow in *Heart of Darkness.* He speaks for the whole book like a siege, such a prick, even though he's not even the narrator. If Sanjay asked our names at first it was for their use as interjection, as he told us about that ship so insignificant in the whole ocean going down. "You know what, Kristen, it really did, man."

KRISTEN – HENRY

I busted my tendon in Dresden (in 2009) because I picked up both packs with one arm (Henry was sleeping). Because the night before, he had relapsed at an electronics festival. The owner of this hostel was looking at me like I'm feeble and so thin and maybe I'm an abused woman at least or taken, a taken person with her gangly American boyfriend leaving like that in the middle of the night against the rules to participate in the streets and taking free drinks, and pills, leaving her place at 3 AM breaking the rule (a hostel curfew, and he threw his shoe at a door) and the rule about staying clean. She waited for our packs to be picked up. She looked at my arms. Because our stay was over. We had seen Dachau what the fuck we had gone to the festival, boozelessly dancing like idiots. It was time to go. I wanted to show her I could handle these things, myself and I can handle this, that he left and now this incessant sleeping, in every hostel, and I could not wake him (his heart was beating) so I picked up two enormous packs with one arm, and my tendon.

Kristen was subletting the apartment. A photograph appeared on the internet of her in Montana wearing all of my jewelry at once, in our apartment. You shouldn't charge a good friend to stay like that in your home. Why did I sublet to such a person? She left the apartment wholeheartedly (for me) cleaner than we could keep it.

REBECCA

In New York I saw Rebecca. She was living in a slim Williamsburg hallway for 700 dollars a month. Her good friend from Bard was renting it to her at that price and kept two back bedrooms for herself, and her art. A photographer. A video artist. She made limited edition DVDs of her experiments and, in the room she didn't sleep in, knitted cases for DVDs if she sold these, like, it comes with my knitting a craft so opposite to my industrial art this disc. I was staying with them a little, before moving into the loft of my rich ex in Philadelphia. Rebecca was working in two restaurants and dating a man who dated. I met them at a bar. They were on some cocaine. He reached out and touched my crotch. A clothed cunt is a crotch? With the back of one of his fingers. He looked smooth, jellied, fished up from the very scrim of his very good website. She laughed into his shoulder, an unbelievable barfly my good friend was becoming, like crinkling a butterfly. Balling it.

My friend for some time. She did not come back to her hallway and I slept there for another night. Her miraculous tea tree face oil. Rebecca, adept at eBay sales. I liked it the dignity in not doing shit for me.

I had gone to the bar only to write. They'd showed up, drunk. When her man touched my crotch, I didn't think, "I like this." I couldn't throw him off though, or make a big point. I was a dependent, the guest. My home in Montana crumpled like that a hysterical inflatable castle and her man (a musician, he maintained a very oily website so you could slide the pictures of himself right around) estimated the wayward position of my pant-swaddled cunt (like a butterfly on crutches) and he reached out, because really I was like a homeless woman. He held Rebecca thoroughly by her slim waist while he did it, it was her roomlessness. Her hallway that led to such nonsense.

PHOTOGRAPHY + KRISTEN + SPECULUM

I told Kristen what it was like those months in Aramingo when I met her at last in Málaga. *At last*. I was relieved. Off the bus. There were so many flowers, dripping and extending off everything, full of neon thrombosis. This woman had founded with Iván, her husband, this residency program, I told Kristen, and it was *her*, she had smashed that large mirror at Manuel's. She came in. It was nuts. They lived somewhere else, with their sweet daughter. It was like a horror film, her disdain for the artists her guests, she hated it, hated time, life, an artist's time. Or she wasn't on her medicine (because she was breastfeeding). I was on Frenadol.

She had extended in her manner a theater of appreciation for all things. She often seemed dewy with the dawning of: a fascist gratitude. It dominated. It shamed. She often extended the affect of childlike wonder at the world (a flower, her daughter) in a way that made me think: there is money. She extended her arm out of the window of a moving vehicle and at the olive trees on the hill had said in a murmur, "Muy trico." She taught me that word with a sumptuous smile.

I didn't want to know it, *trico*, to italicize experience or Spanish or to be moved by vehicle. I was in the back seat with Susana, who looked impatient, bored. That is correct. But a guest should be eager, the enthusiast, compliant and linguistically a porous person if foreign. I thought my money (my decapitated CD) would excuse me a little. I was not so much a leech but a paying person so does a little money excuse me from being curious or reflectively sumptuous a speculum? But really a woman is always the guest, and a woman who is less the guest (if there are two or more women, as there were here: Susana was there) will guest the shit out of the woman who has less bearing, so as to get some fucking footing for herself, and walk like a man a little bit, a little breath, on the bones and the guest-labor of the other. This was *this*. "Muy trico," she told me like I gave a shit, like I wanted to receive a lesson—a bildungsromañero—"It means rich," she said, she interjected, and said my name, "like something is just very very rich."

I listened enough to nod. I complied, and smiled. I was trying to write a novel about Pennsylvania, and English. About language that used me but you can use it. You can write. A writer isn't a receptacle, is actually a big reptile. Or small. I wrote at my desk, the dining table. They would walk into Manuel's and gather me for rides through their country, the longest ways from place to place. *Muy trico.* The olive trees, the sheep there, the sun even, the falabella by the cow, none of it was rich to this paying artist, none dense and full like that at all but hollow, surfaces I only suffered to stuff with otherous content. Something else was going on.

I don't think they saw what they had really begun.

In Seville, I told Kristen about this dewy affect I had endured and how it infuriated. We photographed each other with Kristen's camera looking like that, a joke, mocking her, looking appreciative, dawning like that with a dewy wonder in Seville in its parks, restaurants, looking at dogs on balconies like that, at dog shit, churches of ballooning stones, and many paintings. A whole series.

I photographed Kristen in front of a painting of a rotund, blonde woman a speculum, somewhere hanging in a palace garden. I insisted she pose there. She smiled sheepishly allowing me to see these things—to have had her here, in life, will expand my death.

SANJAY

The sun was setting and it wasn't at all boring. There was a place you could go to in what Sanjay was saying. He talked forever and it was boring, but we didn't have to listen. No one is listening to Marlow (in *Heart of Darkness*, not while he talks out the whole book), they're all sleeping on that lonesome yawl waiting only to go home to London and Joseph Conrad wrote it. He put them asleep, it was him. They're asleep before Marlow even begins. Marlow is boring and Conrad isn't boring (isn't Marlow) because he kills the whole thing his whole serialized publication with the explicit prospect of untold, nearby, concurrent, and probably better dreams.

You have to dream like that when a man begins to *Heart of Darkness* your whole goddamn time, when he publishes himself on the backs of your nodding face, for hours. The sun was setting. I drifted off, nodding. I let Kristen do some of the listening the more punctual nodding. She spaced out. I watched the sunset and then came back around. I took the reins. I said, "Ok, Sanjay, so what happened?"

SHERVIN

"Kriisten," he said.

He stopped us on the street and she jumped. I did. So he was there, too, in Granada. And he was good looking, better than anyone I'd seen in months, maybe more than Ángel, sure, leaner and younger with an evil tilt in his hips, a nice shirt. The shirt of an irresistible narcissist. He had a bone-roughened face cohered with intelligence, dash of tangerine in the brown. It was gorgeous. He was talking to her, imploring her to come with him, with one of his feet on the small curving road, the cobblestones, so that he could be killed or maimed at any moment. Elegant like that. Controlling time, curving Spain.

At the hostel later I felt I had to masturbate in tribute to a person like this. Not so Spanish. How he had said, "Kriisten."

But I didn't masturbate in our room.

We read each other stories we'd written, one line from each thing switching so they intertwined. Hers was a true story on him. He had stolen her friend's scarf in Norway, from a coat pile at a party. He denied it but he had it—the sexual biter—later back at his place (they had such sex), a floating banner of wool.

ÁNGEL + SUSANA

Ángel knew Susana from someplace else, years ago. They fought and he sat in the salon silent while she moved herself about Manuel's vehemently. She packed her cameras and papers for the convent. She would go up. There was not even toilet paper. I heated tea in a cracked glass carafe on the stovetop if a lighter was around. The glass was cracked but intact enough. I stockpiled new packs of lighters in my room, if the store was open I had bought these, but if Susana needed to smoke and her lighters (all of the stove's, each one) were up at the convent and it was night, the stars like the scat of odalisque deer, I fed them to her, one by one whenever. I was hers. I was her friend. Mostly, the stove was unusable, a site of indelible lighterlessness, this cold box and the oven had never worked, and the lighters all floated as balloons (balloons, come into this)—they came in packs of reds, greens, blues—up to the convent like magnets. Ok, what comes cold? Unpasteurized milk lasted for weeks in Manuel's refrigerator. Glug, glug. Blood sausage is cured, good. And Frenadol is fine, works in my fingers, if you put it in water.

I don't know what they were fighting about. They had gone up once, to the convent in the middle of the night, to watch *Soudain le vide* on the projector. There suddenly was one. I wondered if they couldn't have each other. Was it this? Had she wanted it? Had he wanted to film a plastic bag and cat's near interest in this, the ocean, or the shoe, for hours?

Maybe he had said something to her about Bruno but had not offered up a beautiful alternative.

IT WAS RAINING

Flaubert is mean to Emma Bovary. I mean, he kills her.

I took it personally. I couldn't understand why he spent his whole book like that, mocking her. For wanting? How cruel, I thought.

Emma swollen with wants and he kicks her. He actually kills her. It's not fair. It's fair to want. She takes pills like Henry it kills her.

He lives in Atlanta. He teaches college and works with veterans.

I thought, Flaubert, you abuse. You make a woman so silly and what can she do? You punish her for wanting anything, but desire goes where it can, man. It can't leave. Where could she go?

I couldn't separate myself from Emma on the balcony. I felt so insulted, alone like that, without what: the Spanish language or a little company, hot water, a warm house, a lighter or my computer. The rain was coming like stream pellets like river bullet points boinging on Manuel's table out there, off his room. Coming in. It was enough to go inside, into that showerless shivering house. Three stories. The marble floors to keep everyone cool though winter is more real in Spain than the collective Spaniard imagination of the temperature. An insistent memory of summers. It's almost a wholly blanketless country. Nobody stockpiles any blankets or has them, simply, in a closet. Rarely heaters in any house. There were old sheets. They were Manuel's. Old and hard, time does not soften much. They were older and harder still to have outlived him like parrots outliving us or the turtles and the books, his rough sheets. I only shivered under them, effective as newspapers. Not good.

It was raining so hard I went in. No one had arrived yet, even Susana who would keep the house whatever this means, and no shower yet. One burner was working, the oven was always dead.

Maybe even when Manuel was alive. The rain filled the stream and made the castle recede, blanketed (the only blanket I ever encountered there) in a pigeon-spritzing mist. The big gray comforter.

I finished *Madame Bovary* off, like a sour bottle of something, nothing else in the house. I watched like a film the death of her, the desperation she finally felt. Emma was so done, man. It's not nice. He plays with her corpse for some time. The book doesn't end but she dies and he plays with the corpse the name still. I adore him now, playing like that with the dead novel, saying it's dead, animating it so that it looked so dead and more articulated as such, a death. He plays with his death.

JEAN-PHILLIPE

What would I say to him? Should I write to Jean-Phillipe Toussaint, the Belgian writer, what, a little email?

In his book he has a fangirl who follows him around. A professor (a man) arranges for this meeting but they shove her off—"scram"—when what they want is to be left alone, to be just men, and to go to a strip club. It's an extra-permissive place on the Asian continent and you, for instance, can even put your fingers into the pussy of the attendant.

I hate Toussaint. I hate his writing. It has all the restraint of good writing pooling all the restraint and commanding it, to restrain, what you or I could do, too, if want for what we ever write was waiting for us like that, with calm and open affirmation, for whatever we produce, the produce of our first wrist. But it's not like that. I have to shill off many wrists to find any place. It's like suicide. Any place at all. Toussaint, he publishes with what Dalkey Archive Press?

You can write anything, good restrained writing like his, into the pussy the cushioned hole of having a publisher. He has his fingers up the attendant's cunt. It's more interesting for him than the fan who was following them around, that girl-duckling, a sheepette. They ditch her, him and the professor. Raison d'écrire, to shill women. Go on, spend my time. Women are like that, waiting rooms for royalty checks.

I *am* restraining myself. Work without hope. These are my best restraints.

ARAMINGO + PUPPY + SUSANA + BUS

What is art what?

To get open? For what? I don't want that world in me.

The world is dead, must I love you until I am?

My field was inoffensive, unferromagnetic. People stopped approaching *at last*. They didn't show up any longer to Manuel's or invite me. The square was theirs, I looked for plugs that worked. I looked at ants their skin stretched with high plum like cherry teardrops (powerful, crawling) of the very sun crying if you watch them colonize at noon.

I didn't open myself to learning any Spanish. I learned when Susana would wake, and I listened for her vehemence in packing, going back up, where I stopped going. Never. Fleas. I prayed she wouldn't bring them back down with her. They did stay dutifully with that pup. Would she die of it? Would this hippy negligence, this excuse, come to a murder?

I found Susana. I used my casualest voice and put my hand like a visor over my beady eyes: "Hey. Um. Before you head up. Can you untwist this?"

She did, if she could.

She said goodbye to me. Others were at the convent, or napping or had left for New York with our funds, the convent languishing with little light, one or two chairs about. The parched plot. Potatoes dying inside the world. I went to the wrong bus stop—where they said—by myself. She told me she would cry so go. She pushed me off, like a dinghy.

But she was open that was her art, the dilation of her camera (at night). Like relaxing a sphincter the camera staying open like that for such a long time. Perilous openness—but what can you do with it?

She turned the castle into a picture of her patience the

protraction of her extreme vulnerability, staying still like that at night on a hill, alone. Woman. The moon, the moon. She patiently, and without pointing at it, collected it.

A photographer is like that. You stay where you are. A writer, just write on the bus.

NIPPLE

At the retirement party, people made speeches until my mom hollered from her wheelchair, "I feel like I get to hear my own funeral!" Her friend, her best friend for a long time, addressed me after the speeches, in front of people at the table, lunch at an inn: "You always knew what was going on. You knew what he was and we kept trying but you saw what was going on from a very young age. You knew it before us, and you took it. Beatings for your knowledge."

My sister heard it. She got up. She couldn't hear it.

And here I was imagining this woman, my mother's best friend, had thought the worst of me, the way I had acted out. I raged and slumped and scowled as a child. I'd Bartleby'd and Cassandra'd and wailed. This horrible king. Monster-father.

Are you reading this?

You threw that chair. You touched my nipple.

You didn't love—you didn't give love—to my sick mother.

VAULT + ÁNGEL + BRUNO + PHOTOGRAPHY + I AXED THE PIG HEAD

My dad traumatized by the Holocaust, a vast, glowing vault? Henry, the addict, his bad family? Alcoholics all of them? That fleabitten human being, what like a puppy? Really was he a child?

A woman doesn't have time to make up an understanding.

She needs her energies (all of them) to leave. Ángel, in Aramingo, he was ok. He did his work (he filmed an old shoe I showed him because it was like a modern peasant's shoe, from the Van Gogh painting the grooves vibrant with rot, destroyed on the roadside, the sun articulating the pale blue burst of it, the kidney tenderness of that shoe there, under hay and dirt) and he was not pulled around, taken on dates and drives. No one taught him, or thought of what he'd learn. No one asked him to undress and wear their little daughter's see-through slip. He was wearing a suit, like a ghost. A man is like that, a ghost, something you wouldn't touch. It was freezing. Bruno led me to the butcher's freezer, to the photographer who would be waiting for us there. And he warned me, everyone was so exhausted with me, "Just relax. Try to have fun. Be open." He gave me a little roadside lesson before we went in. In the beginning I had axed the pig head, but they'd forgotten. It had lost currency completely. Now I seemed incredibly un-immersed. Hostile even, or sullen. A woman should leave. That's what artists do, isn't that right, Toussaint?

SAMUEL

Four years later I wrote to Samuel. I put in his letter a beeswax chip from a used-up candle (because it smells like pussy + duck fat) and one of the woodchips from out front which had been (in Salt Lake, all spring these guys) the conductive sequins of the sunset on the high rim of a canyon, and *The Lover*.

I wrote to Samuel four years since I had from Spain, when I implored him to join me in Aramingo—I hadn't said then, tactically, anything about the fleas, and I borrowed language from the website about what it was like, because I wanted what to fuck. I didn't want to write.

Now I was in Utah four years later. What the fuck. I wrote to Samuel wanting an invitation to Amsterdam. I thought he was there. To test our fake love letters even then though they weren't real and in fact embarrassed us greatly. It shamed.

Henry had left our place. I'd been with him since Spain (off and on) while both his parents died (in two years). I went to hospice and memorial service, to California very frequently. My whole Christmas one year (his mom's death) was warm. And I kept coming onto the glistening asphalt in a plane, the hosed tarmac with schmears of diamonds. To meet my love, I loved him irresolvably— you would, his lips the plum-amphibium, the joy that could crack out of there—and to go over things. There were things to take. He took her OxyContin. We took her Dyson vacuum.

And then he relapsed in Salt Lake and I was alone with these woodchips—the sun coming at their jugular, each thing has a jugular. I thought: Samuel.

That letter took a month to arrive at his old address (to a residency that was paying him). He had moved off but returned months later (because they wanted to pay him again) and they gave it to him, in the residency office, such an old package now with *The Lover* dead inside. I heard from him a month after that, when I was leaving Salt Lake, with a stone, and his letter. He had broken up with someone. He had been with her this whole time, since and before our bad commission in 2011. Now he was on a train, and later—the letter continued to be made—in his bed the letters slurred—I loved it, my love for Samuel.

Something is real?

He had written (to Spain, after the commission had ended in shame): I have a girlfriend. She's incredible: the most open, friendly, easygoing person I know. We'll bump into someone on the street, and straight away she's into a conversation, inviting them for a coffee, whatever, while I stand there, a feeling of dread swelling in my gut, my jaw clenching, just wanting it to be over, to come through it unscathed (not because I don't want to know that person but, on the contrary, because I want to know them *so badly* but have no idea how to go about it).

I moved again. I abandoned my books there. I don't speak

with Henry. I have Samuel's letter, and stone.

It did not occur to me (at all) that a woodchip would not carry with it what it had been. My deep incuriosity—I wasn't curious—it was. The sunset—the canyon rim wearing, like a shy sheep someone dressed, a wreath of birds. And a book, if you read it and then send it, isn't it embroidered in how you were? There are things. You think a book (out of all of them) resuscitates.

SHEEP + VERA

When we came back into town it was night and there was a festival. The speakers had been hauled out and old men sat around in pants anti-fuchsia, anti-violet, tan polyester or darker. They were delighted we had arrived, casual on our bikes. We had rolled up, like we were part of the town and had come. We walked around and talked to whoever bade us, they winked, to come sit near their knees, and let our cheeks be kissed a little long. I had a feeling in Aramingo of the acute impossibility of rape. Everything inappropriate was mild and persistent. You couldn't ever say you were leaving. No one would understand. You developed techniques. You bade no adieus.

You just left.

WHITE MATERIAL

She has a son she can't stand. An idle loaf of white flesh by the pool. They have a pool. Her hands—Isabelle Huppert's—an acting orchard out of her. Her husband is very French (not so good).

She is committed to living in Africa, being on the black moon like this and somehow surviving. She ignores many problems. She persists in operating her family's, her father's, old coffee plantation. She arranges for new men to wash their beans while others are dropping out, leaving, afraid, fighting. She only persists.

Violence starts to cloak the film. There are guns with men, in a Cameroon that can't be like that anymore. They can't like her.

I watched it in Manuel's salon, and put my hand on the table, to do something, to give gesture to the feeling of being. I could have touched anything. I held on.

White and even light gray stones on the ground, picked up, are because the moon has cried, and exploded? I slept under Manuel's white sheets to collect it, the moon, the drapes open. There is the moon, object resonance unto this (the sheet like a magnet, a magnetic basket. Open the drapes). It walks on us. Not the other way around, like *The Shining*. A brilliant film walks all over you.

JEAN-PAUL

In Philadelphia I met Jean-Paul through OkCupid. My sandal that I had since Cordoba, hauling out that good Spanish leather simple without embellishments (fuck American footwear, for women you go too far. *It's too far.*)—it snapped. On the street it just did and I met him with it fangled to my foot, so to still walk on its base (to a bar, to get a little drunk).

Feeling poor for winter, I ordered cheap boots made so far afield of my feelings, my tenderness, and they arrived via Pakistan too small but I wore them persistent in being poor like that, the kind of person who just makes it fit. They hurt me immensely. The nerves burst in both foot-tops and I wore toe-separating socks manufactured in the US to bed, with Jean-Paul.

In the shower, he dropped soap on my foot, on one of the burst nerves, a pink curved Dove bar like a UFO of pig fat. But I knew what this was. It was hurtful, and it happened again the next week, to the same foot, and the same foot that my sandal snapped from, suddenly, when I was walking to meet him crossing Osage Avenue.

We discussed in the shower my belief that *twice* = Something, so here it is, twice this attack, Jean-Paul, so why is this soap hitting my foot?

That book by Ponge is called *Le savon*. I finally remembered.

At the bar, we sat in a corner so dark in the afternoon, off the window. Gaston Bachelard the phenomenologist (for whom reasons are draining) knows corners as germs of dreams. We clicked. Things snap. I have moved from man to man. I can't find work.

MURAT

Murat was always clothed, it seemed he had passed out. A spontaneous sleep, unplanned. He hadn't tucked himself in. He lay on his stomach on the bunk in this hostel, at a slant above the sheets. It was the best place: the beach below if you walked a cyclone of streets down. On the beach: fires in cans, a dog the hair curled like a bashful little bush of payots, and flowers the pink whipped with lashes of tangerine and fuchsia spattered, a high fruit pox.

We always had to whisper in our room in that cheerful hostel. Murat was on his bed, dressed and sleeping, on his stomach on a slant as if he had just fallen. We had to be so quiet, at all hours. He was always there, asleep.

I wondered if he was ill. I constructed a narrative that this was his last trip walking, anything, before he'd be wheelchair confined, and in other ways done. My mom like that so suddenly the falling woman, snapped off the vertical rails, and in bushes sometimes I saw her on the front walk, and asleep much. She called me when she woke, for Cokes. She wanted, always, three pieces of ice. I came bounding out of my room (I was writing). A pen is a little oar in a roaring ocean, but you don't have the other one.

I wondered what Murat might have come down with. Was this MS, an autoimmune issue this extreme display of exhaustion, or boredom? Was it depression? He told me, art school had been such bullshit for him. There was no life in it. I kept up the tiptoeing but Kristen talked at full volume suddenly (she was done) and played a recorder and moved with ease and candor and daytime attitudes through the small shared room. We knew she'd lose her parasol at some point but she still had it. She called to it, "Mi Parasol." I told her, "Shh," but she was really done. There is a limit. There's a limit to being quiet. And he slept anyway, a dreamer against this experience. I spoke now at full volume also. We had to maneuver at full level. We had to communicate about trains and the wedding. Tickets, times, and deals. We disrobed in front of his back, the face obscure. It wasn't a problem. When he woke up and talked, I thought, "It's surprising." He talked the whole time. Not surprising. I listened. But he didn't tell me about his illness, narcolepsy maybe, or MS. I don't know why he slept so much. I didn't consider he was taking heroin. I've always thought: "I do not think it is that."

SHEEP

My body weakened as entirely as it can and still keep its bones. But the bones showed their underbellies of gelatin. I slumped.

The air was hot and static, the olive trees like stencils of trees. We had only just begun our ride. I did not know Vera. I did not know why this upset her so. A thought is so powerful, I thought, so *so what?*

On the hill, when we'd ascended enough and found this place by a farmhouse, its occupants all asnooze (I went in and took their knife), the sun was aging like a balzac irredeemably wrinkling on the horizon. And then, the afternoon reached further (there's more), producing a castration of a ball slung and oozing down the hill, and I thought: "Fainting rejuvenates me. I feel, when a thought touches me, and slings me down like a fool, reborn." The proof: my heart was more even then in its beating than it has ever even been, like a red sheep in a pasture with all the others, black and white and tan. The red one is shy, warm, and cunning like a moving bush of fraying (I guess used) tampons.

JEAN-PAUL + NIPPLES – SPAIN

In his apartment, secretly encrusted with dear and well-spaced (many hidden) totems, he said, "Do you like biting?" He bit me all over on my chest and neck. He bit my nipples intensely. He said, "I don't want to hurt. I want to feel what's there."

It aroused me immensely, to hear want. To bear his. I thought about Shervin, and Kristen. I thought I had really joined something. A biting sex cult. I thought of Spain. The bite on her neck, I too had wanted one. The bites kept coming, all through first sex with Jean-Paul (Marius, Hyppolite . . .)—look, there's a Tibetan bat carved from bone. Rosewood tonsu. Look. Piece of spine.

I saw my mother later, in the morning. She hollered from her scooter, "Why are you glowing!"

The flea bites marred my back + stomach for years. They were dark like daguerreotypes of black nipples on me, spattered. Dr. Money ceases to email. In my last response I offered to send him a copy of my book, what I'd talked of writing while in Spain, on the plane home, what I'd hoped I'd publish and I have, and traditionally, when you offer your work, a free book, this stops correspondences, yes? I don't know where Rebecca is. You can't get Frenadol. The residency program, in its fifth year of operation, lists many artists on its site, hundreds from around the globe who have been there since the prototype: me, small, at Manuel's, in his bed, like a human seed, and bitter. I left *Madame Bovary* there, and Roberto Bolaño's *The Savage Detectives*, but took *L'espace littéraire* only to leave it like a lot in Salt Lake, the Ponge to Ángel. He emails, he mass emails, quotes.

"The world is gone, I must carry you."

"I will love you until I'm dead."

The artists, I see, in a sliding scroll of website photographs, have covered the convent in sticks and silk, have felted cocoons, have knitted footsteps onto the labyrinthine path, are pictured eating potatoes a kind of burlap fruit, sitting together like a chain in the sun, so what retains?

They are making the world soft.

ARAMINGO

"Hola."

"Hola."

Heron steam ironing the horizon.

"Adio."

"Adio."

ACKNOWLEDGMENTS

For Kristen Jean Gleason and Jean-Paul Cauvin.

Thank you, Caryl Pagel, Hilary Plum, Zach Savich, Danny Khalastchi, Alyssa Perry, Annie Leue, Sevy Perez, Steen Haugsted, Zach Isom, and all others making Rescue. You've loved *Spain* with incredible intelligence, care, and prowess, too. I'm very lucky.

I have quoted from Michael Hamburger's translation of Celan's poem and John Lambert's translation of Jean-Phillipe Toussaint's book. The Duras translation is mine.

This manuscript—like a lot of spirited manuscripts out there—came out of Kathryn Bond Stockton's Canonical Perversions course at the University of Utah, which I still have all over me. My professors Melanie Rae Thon, Lance Olsen, Craig Dworkin, and Deirdre McNamer have challenged and guided me well and are extraordinary.

A special thanks to my students at the University of the Arts in Philadelphia, whom I held in mind as an audience as I wrote (because you were awesome, and already out ahead of me), and to colleagues who cheered me. Thanks, as well, to my students and colleagues at MCLA, whom I will just be meeting and getting to know better by the time this arrives.

Thank you, Brian Blanchfield, Chris Kraus, and Vi Khi Nao—your sparkling names—your astounding work somehow—on my book!

And here's to writer friends, reasons for sticking around (many mentioned above): Jessica Alexander, Rachel Levy, Raphael Dagold, Meg Day, Aaron Shulman, Joanna Ruocco, Lisa Schumaier, Brandon Shimoda, Anne Marie Wirth Cauchon, Phil Baber, Nabil Kashyap, Steven Dunn, Jacob Kahn, Tessa Fontaine . . .

Caren Beilin is the author of a novel, *The University of Pennsylvania* (Noemi Press, 2014), and a collection of short fictions, *Americans, Guests, or Us* (New Michigan Press, 2012). She teaches creative writing at Massachusetts College of Liberal Arts.

RESCUE PRESS

OPEN PROSE SERIES

edited by Hilary Plum and Zach Savich

Anne Germanacos, *Tribute* (2014)
Christian TeBordo, *Toughlahoma* (2015)
Erik Anderson, *Estranger* (2016)
Andrea Lawlor, *Paul Takes the Form of a Mortal Girl* (2017)
Caren Beilin, *Spain* (2018)

RESCUEPRESS.CO